VIETAM: THERE AND BACK

©2018 Jim Purtell

Published by Hellgate Press

(An imprint of L&R Publishing, LLC)

Hellgate Press

PO Box 3531

Ashland, OR 97520

email: info@hellgatepress.com

Cover Design: LeAnn Zotta and Colleen Miller

Interior Design: L. Redding

Cataloging In Publication Data is available from the publisher upon request.

ISBN: 978-1-55571-901-2

Printed and bound in the United States of America

First edition 10 9 8 7 6 5 4 3 2 1

For all the soldiers we lost in Charlie Co. 1/6th 198th Light Infantry Brigade from February 1968 to February 1969.

For all infantrymen who have carried the scars of battle from all the wars that the U.S. has been involved in.

For all who lost their lives in the Vietnam War.

Contents

PART THREE

VIETNAM
THERE & BACK

*A Combat
Medic's Chronicle*

JIM "DOC" PURTELL

HELLGATE PRESS   ASHLAND, OREGON

Acknowledgments

A FTER WRITING THE INITIAL DRAFT OF THIS MEMOIR, I sent it to Al Torsiello, my platoon mate with whom I served in Vietnam. He read it and, without telling me, allowed a friend of his, a university instructor, to read it. His friend liked it, saying that he thought it was "honest and authentic." However, he suggested that I find an editor.

Because his recommendation made sense to me, I spent time thinking about people I know whom I would trust with my story. I decided to approach Barbara Wuest, the wife of a long-time friend. Since Barbara is a former English/Writing professor and a poet, I thought she might be able to help me out with the editing. Thankfully, she agreed. After numerous edits, she was able to make the sentences more clear and therefore easier to read. What I am most grateful for is that she was able to make needed changes without eviscerating my voice.

I also want to thank Al Torsiello who read several different drafts. Not only did he serve as an excellent sounding board but he also wrote the Foreword. For both, I am truly grateful. He and I have been friends since we met in the jungles of Vietnam and will be friends to the end.

Another good friend, Rudy Cardin, was also instrumental in the making of this book. Rudy went through medical training with me at Fort Sam Houston in 1967. He and I also went through

Vietnam orientation together in Chu Lai in February 1968. He served as a combat medic with an infantry outfit. After reading my story (in one sitting), he told me that my experience was also his experience. Because he understood my story as well as he did, he was able to make valuable recommendations for changes that I ended up adopting.

Finally, I want to thank Mary Nigl, my girlfriend of many years, who read the book and enthusiastically encouraged me to publish it.

Foreword

NOT MANY GOOD THINGS COME OUT OF WAR, but for me a close friendship with Jim "Doc" Purtell is one. Doc (as he would be known to this day by anyone who served in combat with him) became my friend in February 1968 when he stepped off of a chopper in the jungles of Vietnam. He was there to replace our former medic whom we had lost in combat a few weeks earlier. I'd been in country only a few weeks myself, and we bonded immediately. Doc was a medic, not trained for combat like the rest of the men he served with; but when the shit hit the fan, we could always count on him. No one he served with would dispute that.

We fought together for most of our time in country and shared all the same experiences, which turned out to be what we both feel was our way of coping with the aftermath of the war once we were home. I never thought anyone who hadn't been there with me would believe my stories. In fact, my wife of over 40 years has heard none of my war experiences. It was only with Doc that I was able to discuss the things that happened to us in Vietnam.

I was home from the war for a few years and only just starting to experience the effects of PTSD, but not knowing what it was. I hadn't seen or heard from Doc since we got home from Vietnam. Then about six years later, he turned up on my doorstep, and we started telling each other about how we were feeling. We both feel that these talks are what kept us sane through the aftermath of our war experience. I highly recommend this book to other combat veterans as well as their family and friends. It could be a good way for other veterans, who come home from war feeling lost and confused, to see that they are not alone, that many others are going through the same difficulties of assimilating back into society.

Although Doc and I live in different parts of the country, we still see each other and speak on a regular basis. We don't always talk about Vietnam but it still comes up, and it's still good to know there is someone to rely on when the old demons emerge.

Alan Torsiello Charlie Company
1st Battalion 6th infantry Americal Division
Feb. 1968 to Feb. 1969

Preface

WHEN I WAS A YOUNG BOY, I was an eager reader who consumed biographies of famous Americans. I also read several historical novels, but the one that I read and re-read several times was Steven Crane's *Red Badge of Courage*. I was struck by the stark realism of war in that book. It was like nothing else I had read at the time. The author did such an amazing job of pulling the reader into the scenes that I could easily imagine being there participating in the war effort. I never dreamed at that time that I would actually be exposed to so many of the situations that I'd read about as a young boy, the struggle between self-interest and group obligations, individual survival, courage, manhood, honor, maturity and mortality.

****

It was 1968, one of the worst years in American history since the Civil War. The country had already buried Martin Luther King, Jr. in April and Robert Kennedy in June, both reportedly murdered by lone assassins. And I was in one of the most dangerous places in the world, during the worst time of the Vietnam War, on top of a hill in the Central Highland with only about twenty-five other guys. We were in foxholes we had dug hours before, and the night was eerily quiet.

We'd been hit so hard in previous months that we were told to avoid encountering the enemy, to the extent possible, because our numbers had grown dangerously small. The still of the very dark night was broken by hand grenades thrown from positions directly below us. The enemy was so close to us that our lieutenant called for gunships. He thought we were so exposed and vulnerable that we'd all be overrun and killed. Afraid for my life, I desperately longed for the safety of my home back in the States where I was born nineteen years earlier.

PART ONE

Growing Up
in the Midwest

I WAS A WILD KID. ACCORDING TO MY MOTHER, I was born with a vivid imagination and a very independent streak. I grew up in a rural area with eleven brothers and sisters. Back in the '50s, families in general were larger than they are today. So, besides having my siblings all around, I also had plenty of neighborhood kids to hang out with. We'd often get on our bikes and race around the local streets. Sometimes we'd stop and raid the neighbor's currant patch or stop at a fort we'd built in a nearby wooded area. Back then, before computers and cell phones, we entertained ourselves. We usually had enough players to form teams for a baseball, basketball or football game, depending on the season. We'd often play for hours and hours until we had to go home for meals or for the evening.

When I went home after playing all day, I could count on my father being there ruling the roost with an iron fist. Later in life, I began to better understand why he was such a strict disciplinarian. Back in the '40s, long before women's liberation, my father had to become the "man" of the family. He had three older sisters and an older brother, Tom. When Tom was younger, he had been accidentally hit in the head with a wooden bat in a pick-up baseball game. Because of this accident, he needed care for the rest of his life; and my father was the one who had to look after him. When Tom would disappear from the house, my father was always the one called upon to search for him. Often the only way he could find Tom was with the help of the police. My father became resourceful at an early age. He developed a very aggressive manner about him, a manner that instilled fear in most if not all of his own children.

In my early years, I was very afraid of my father. After all, he was the one who administered the punishment in the family. Giving time-outs or putting a kid in the corner were not forms of punishment used in the '50s, at least not in our household. We did get our share of spankings, though. For me and my brother, Dic, the spankings started first with a bare hand on the buttocks. It then graduated to belts. When the belts were worn out, he used double-edged razor straps on the buttocks and upper legs. It's likely that, today, this type of punishment would constitute child abuse.

In my teen years, I got into more than my share of trouble. The more juvenile acts I committed the harder my father was on me. Because I had become a very fit, tough and strong teenager, the punishment changed from physical to mental. For example, he would make me copy in long hand several pages of small print from the classified section of our local newspaper. It would take me hours to finish. If my father found a single mistake—and he always did, be it a misspelling, an omitted punctuation mark or word—he would rip the pages and throw them on the floor. Then, I had to do the whole thing over. This happened to me numerous times.

Once, in my early teens, we kids were playing baseball in our yard. When I got up to bat, I accidentally hit my younger brother Bill's forehead as I was bringing my wooden bat back. Bill was inexperienced and, as the catcher, too close to the batter. As a result of this incident, I had to spend a week during the summer in the foyer sitting on a chair during my waking hours. Not only did I have to take my meals there alone, but my siblings were told not to speak to me. I wasn't even allowed to have anything to read or look at but the foyer itself. I was supposed to just sit there and think about what I had done. Believe me, I had done a lot of things that I should have been disciplined for, but this was an accident, not something I did deliberately. In my father's defense, however, I understand now that his overreaction may have to do with his own brother's head injury that resulted in learning and social disabilities that ruined his life. I get this now; but at the time, I felt I had been punished unjustly.

Despite the difficulty I had enduring my father's harsh discipline, I was still cocky and rebellious in high school. Having observed my older brothers before they moved on to more mature activities, I stepped in and assumed their leadership positions in our neighborhood group. Although I wasn't conscious of it at the time, I was much more of a leader than a follower. As a result, over time, I was elected vice president of my freshman homeroom and president of my homeroom class in my sophomore, junior and senior years. Also, in Catholic grade school and high school, I played basketball and football, enjoying football more because of the physical nature of the game. With good coaching, I developed my skills and became a good athlete. Having been lucky enough to play on some good teams, I received the usual athletic achievement awards.

All of this was interrupted when I was a freshman in high school, which is when one of the most tragic events of my life occurred. The first Irish Catholic President of the United States was assassinated in Dallas shortly after lunch on November 22, 1963. Like most Americans, I remember exactly where I was when I first heard the news. I was at Lourdes High School in

Oshkosh, a school taught by the Christian Brothers. At about 1:00 p.m. CST, Brother Anthony's voice came over the public address speaker telling us that JFK had been shot. A few minutes later, his voice came back on the speaker saying that the President had been killed. He said buses were to arrive in a few minutes. School was closed, and the scheduled basketball game was canceled. Of course, no one cared about the game. Totally devastated, we left school with heavy hearts.

Later that day, my father came home from his dental office with three French-speaking boys about my age in tow. They belonged to a touring French Catholic boys' choir called the Little Singers of Paris. Their concert in our area had been canceled. A call had gone out to community leaders asking them to take these boys in, as there were no rooms to be had in our local hotels. My father answered that call and accepted responsibility for these three boys. The country was paralyzed. So these boys, who couldn't speak a word of English, joined me and my eleven siblings and my parents—seventeen of us altogether—for the entire weekend. Like people throughout the United States, we positioned ourselves around the television and watched the events unfold. The weekend was particularly sad at our house because we were Irish Catholic and enthusiastic supporters of JFK. When the accused assassin Lee Harvey Oswald came into view in the basement of the police department and a man later identified as Jack Ruby shot him, we were all aghast at what we had seen. The French boys recoiled in horror too. Together we had witnessed the first murder on live television in the United States and possibly the world. I felt sorry for these young boys being so far from their home and so did my father. He allowed each of them to call their parents. At that time, long-distance calling, especially to Europe, was very expensive.

So I knew what a generous act this was on my father's part.

To this day I remember vividly not only my father's generosity but also the boys themselves. How strange it must have been for them to be with an American family during this tragic time. Later in life, I hired some French-speaking researchers and tried unsuccessfully to obtain a roster of the Little Singers in Paris. I wanted to know how it was for them to be here with Americans in our time of national mourning.

After these days of grieving, my father resumed his role as the harsh disciplinarian in our household. My need to be independent often conflicted with his need to rule. From the time I was twelve until I turned eighteen, he and I battled. I never won any of these battles. My father was not one to show love in any way. Though his kindness to the French boys might be interpreted as loving, I myself cannot recall ever having strong feelings for him that were returned in any way. Never did I hear the words "I love you" from him when I was growing up. I know I am not alone in this regard. Many people have been raised in a similar way, or far worse. All I know is that, for me, it wasn't the right way.

In 1967, as I was about to graduate from high school, I knew I was not going to go to college. Though I was a fairly good student, I was tired of the academic world. Besides, I was eighteen, which meant I knew all the answers. I was thinking about what I might do when I graduated, but I wasn't doing so very seriously. I was kind of adrift. So, in my senior year, I joined a rock and roll band, a group that I initiated for a talent day in high school with friends Paul Muetzel, John Prescott, Glen Wuest, Tom Thornton and Pete Searles. During the join-up phases of the band, I had to learn bass; so Glen taught me the parts to about forty of their songs, and I muddled my way through playing bass guitar at a very minimal level. Though I played only one or two gigs with them, I really enjoyed it.

Because I was kind of in the band, I traveled with them to

Wausau, Wisconsin, to listen to one of their weekend gigs. On the second night, after the gig, I was defending Pete (the current bass player who would be switching to drums) because a rowdy group of guys in the parking lot wanted to beat him up. I went outside and announced that I was the new bass player and asked the guys sitting on the hoods of their cars what we needed to do about it. A go-go dancer who had been dancing at the club that evening walked outside and tried to persuade these local guys to get in their cars and leave, but her request fell on deaf ears.

The reason they were upset is because one of them had sat in as drummer for both nights for one song. When it was decided that Pete would be the drummer, the guy (who was drunk) got upset. He felt he'd been deliberately upstaged. He directed derogatory, ugly and highly offensive racist remarks toward the Negro go-go dancer. (The terms "African-American" and "black" had not made their way into the mainstream language as yet.) When I verbally corrected him and defended her, the guy called me a "nigger lover" and struck me. One thing led to another, and I got in a major fist fight. The guy sucker-punched me and gave me a black eye, but he got the worst of it. When several of his buddies picked him up from the gravel parking lot and dragged him away, he was bleeding, seemingly, from every part of his body.

Looking back on this incident, I realize that I didn't have to go out in that parking lot when that crowd was calling for Pete to come outside. No one told me to confront them, but I thought I was tough. Since none of my band mates were fighters, I knew we were in a real predicament.

I went out and, in my own way, tried to defuse the situation. The dynamics were such that there was no easy way to resolve the issue. After all, because these guys were local and customers of his, the bar owner wasn't going to call the cops. So I knew we were in big trouble, and we were ninety miles from home. It turns out that the fight did defuse the situation, as the parking lot cleared out shortly after. The owner of the establishment thought we had contributed to the problem and, as a result, docked our pay. Needless to say, it was a quiet ride home that night.

When I got home, it was very late. I made my way to my room and fell asleep. The next morning, unable to hide my black eye, I had to confront my father's anger. He didn't want to hear that I'd defended the go-go dancer and one of the guys in the band. He had no interest at all in my honorable actions. To him, it was just one more incident where I got into trouble. He said, "It's all over for you. You're quitting that band." I told the guys that I could no longer play in the band, which I loved, but I lived in my father's house and had to abide by his rules. After that forced curtailment of my musical career, I vowed then and there that my father would never make another decision that impacted my life. As it turned out, the fight and my father's subsequent punishment were defining events in my life.

I didn't tell my parents that I was thinking about entering the military, but I probably did share it with some of my closer friends near the end of my senior year in high school. I'd observed guys around me who went that route. My friend and neighbor, Bill Lageman, joined the Navy when he graduated from high school to get away from his alcoholic father. After seeing him decked out in his Navy uniform, which I liked, I decided to talk to a Navy recruiter too. Ultimately, I decided I didn't want to spend a lot of time out on a ship in foreign waters.

So I met with a U.S. Army recruiter instead. He fed me a lot of bullshit, and I believed him. The next thing I knew I was signing on the dotted line without telling anyone. The recruiter told me that, based on what I told him about myself, I should be what they called in the Army a "medical aid man." He briefly explained what jobs medics performed. I must have been seeking some approval from my father (who was in the medical profession) because I didn't hesitate to choose the medical field. Furthermore, I had no interest in killing anyone. I preferred to help people.

The recruiter told me I'd work in a nice clean hospital in either Hawaii or Germany, two of the places I'd selected on the enlistment form. When I left that office, I had a good feeling about the recruiter. I thought he was a nice guy. Only later did I learn that recruiters in that era had to fill quotas. The Army would take any able body that walked in their door and could pass the minimum mental and physical requirements.

Since I was eighteen and didn't need parental consent, I kept secret the fact that I joined the Army, that is, until the next flare-up I had with my father. When that happened, I told him he wouldn't have to worry about me anymore because I had joined the U.S. Army and I'd be leaving for basic training after graduation from high school. For the first time in my memory, I saw some fear and apprehension in my father's face. He watched the news every night, so he knew better than I did exactly what was happening in the world, specifically in Vietnam. Because he served in WWII, he was well aware that the decision I made was cause for alarm. He knew I'd made a poor decision, but he never told me so. My mother was very upset. Although my brothers Tom and Tim had left home to go to college, I was the first to leave home to join the military.

After telling my family, I then told my friends and girlfriend. Since they were all aware of my ongoing problems with my father, I guess it was no surprise to them that I made this decision. No one asked me why I was doing this. Looking back, it's obvious to me that I had not thought it through at all. It was an impulsive overreaction on my part. I joined the Army because, at the time, it was the lesser of the evils before me. I didn't want to go to college, and I didn't want to work and live at home. Back in the late '60s, kids didn't get apartments together the way they do now. If young people went to work after graduation, they usually still lived at home with their families until they married. Though I'm sure he didn't see it this way, my father was suffocating me. He became increasingly impossible to live with, so I felt that I had to get away from him at any cost.

While waiting to graduate, I started thinking about the situation I'd gotten myself into. I was aware that our country was involved in a war. Macho that I was, I told my other macho buddies that I wanted to go kill those Viet Cong for the red, white and blue. Some of them even encouraged me, saying I was doing the right thing, but they didn't know any more than I did. It was all false bravado. The truth is, I really knew nothing about Vietnam. Nor did I know anything about killing. In fact, I knew nothing about anything. At that point in my life, I had never really traveled at all. The farthest I'd been away from home was ninety miles. It was 1967. In my town, people my age didn't travel much. If they did, it was by car for the most part.

I graduated from high school in May of 1967, and on or about August 8, 1967, I left home to go to Milwaukee to take my Army physical which I passed with flying colors. Almost everyone passed and, for some reason, I didn't find that odd. It was only later that I realized that the country needed lots of bodies for cannon fodder in Vietnam, so very few people got medical exemptions. The next day, after the physical, I boarded a bus and traveled south toward Ft. Campbell, Kentucky.

Basic Training

O N THAT TRIP SOUTH I DID NOT HAVE A conversation with anyone. The bus was quiet. Almost everyone on board was asleep when we arrived at Fort Campbell at 4:00 a.m. I think having Army recruits arrive at their duty stations very early in the morning is by design, especially for basic training. Once the bus came to stop, the lights came on and two Drill Instructors (DIs) came on the bus and started screaming at us, saying, "You are in our Army now and your asses belong to us." We all scrambled to get off the bus, everyone dazed and sleepy. When I heard one of the DIs ordering us, in bad English, to step up to the yellow line and put our feet together, I had a sinking feeling that I'd made a horrible mistake.

Basic training was tough at that time. It had to be. After all, we were involved in a war that was escalating at a rapid pace under President Johnson. For some reason—and I don't know why—I was selected to be squad leader on the very first day of the actual training cycle. As I look back on this experience, I wonder if racism wasn't involved. I was one of a few white guys in a squad made up mostly of Negroes and Puerto Ricans. It was 1967 and racism was still prevalent back then. Prior to joining the Army, my only experience of different races was playing one basketball game in a state tournament against a Milwaukee school that was made up mostly of minorities. This may be hard to believe; but, except for the go-go dancer at the bar where I got into fight, I had never spoken to a Negro or Hispanic person before going to the Army. They just weren't around where I lived. Most people in my town looked pretty much like me. I'd barely begun my basic training and already I was expanding my horizons.

The first few weeks of our eight-week training cycle involved a lot of physical conditioning, including marching, physical drills and more marching. As a squad leader, I was responsible for seven other guys in my unit. When we were given assignments, I had to see that they were done or I caught a lot of hell from the DIs. I was forced to interact with guys from many different backgrounds, and it was tough. Guys didn't want to follow my instructions, particularly near the end of the training cycle, because they felt that I was a trainee just like them. Sometimes I had to do things by myself, like clean latrines, just to insure that the assignments were completed.

In basic training, we received the same bullshit that guys in the military have received forever. DIs would have us marching, running, climbing and hitting the ground with great regularity. We would have forced marches, bivouac training, rifle drills, KP and every other military-related assignment. The idea was to blend a bunch of undisciplined guys into a cohesive unit so we could become an effective fighting force.

During this time, I didn't make any friends because, in my view, the environment wasn't conducive to friendliness. Many of us were young and scared and away from home for the first time. We were constantly being pushed, which created an atmosphere in which every man felt he was in this for himself. Having been thrown into this together, I suspect we all just did what was necessary to complete the training. Also, we were kept so busy that I found there wasn't enough time for friendships.

Graduation from Basic Training

S EVERAL GUYS HAD FAMILY MEMBERS coming for graduation. I don't recall even talking with my family about graduation. As I saw it, at this point in time, I was completing two months of a thirty-six month enlistment, and I had only just begun. So instead of celebrating with family and friends, I was preparing mentally for the long haul.

On graduation day, everyone was ready and waiting for the ceremony to begin. It seemed that many other guys felt like I did; they just wanted to get it over with and move on. Most of the graduation ceremony was a blur to me, though I recall noticing that our military drill team did a nice job. Also, I remember being disappointed with my own performance. I didn't execute all of my rifle movements as well as I had in practice. I got down on myself; but like I did with everything else in life up to that point, I got through it. After the drill team ceremony, the commanding officer called us one by one. Along with our graduation certificate, we received our military orders for our next assignment.

Next Assignment

A SHORT TIME AFTER THE GRADUATION CEREMONY, we congratulated each other on making it through basic training and talked about our next assignments. Some were going to Ft. Sill, Oklahoma, some staying at Ft. Campbell, others to Ft. Polk, Louisiana, for infantry training. I had orders to go to Ft. Sam Houston, Texas. Collectively, we felt good about the fact that most of the harassment would now be over, and we'd be treated like men in our new assignments. We'd still be soldiers, but we'd no longer be treated like recruits. Before long, we wished each other good luck and said our goodbyes.

At the end of basic training, I learned that several guys had received promotions from pay grade E-1 to E-2; but I didn't. I wasn't happy about it either. After all, I'd been a squad leader and a good one. Then, too, I felt like I'd worked harder than most. Several fellow trainees, who hadn't taken on additional responsibility and work, did get promoted. This meant that they were going to earn more money than I would. I suspected that the reason I stayed E-1 was because I had a personality conflict with one of the DIs. Whatever the reason, I felt like I'd gotten screwed. I was pissed off, to say the least. Other guys in my squad were also shocked that I hadn't been promoted.

So I approached the DI that I had a conflict with and asked why I hadn't received a promotion. He just shrugged his shoulders. Then I asked what the green tag stapled to the top of my orders meant. He said, "I don't know why, but they're sending your ass to leadership school. Somebody must've seen something I didn't see." That was the last time I saw or spoke with that DI. Not getting a promotion put a chip on my shoulder. Actually, my conflict with my father put a chip on my shoulder. This lack of promotion, after all of the hard work and hassles I'd gone through, only added to it.

Leadership Training

L EADERSHIP TRAINING, I SOON LEARNED, was a prep course to teach us how to march trainees around the different areas of the base. This base was not actually a training base in the usual sense. It was for training medical aid men. It was a medical facility on an Army base. Therefore, they needed soldiers who could move the medical corpsman trainees around, and that's what we did. When I graduated from the two-week course, I was given a maroon helmet liner and a black armband with corporal stripes on it and a semi-private room in the barracks. The regular troops wore green helmet liners and stayed in open barracks. One other privilege we had was that we didn't have to wait in long chow lines to eat. We were allowed to go to the front and eat right away so we'd be ready to lead the troops to afternoon sessions. All in all, I was okay with my leadership training and the benefits I received from it.

Advanced Individual Training

I T DIDN'T TAKE LONG FOR ME TO GET INTO the swing of things at Ft. Sam Houston. The pressure and military bearing were not nearly as intense as at Ft. Campbell. For the most part, the bullshit was pretty much gone. The environment was far more relaxed. After all, this was a medical facility. As far as we knew, we were going to be trained to be medics.

In order to be given a military occupational speciality (MOS) and to become a 91A10 medical aid man, we had to complete a number of specific classes and exercises. We were introduced to basic medical equipment and were taught how to identify and use the equipment. We learned how to apply bandages, to set broken limbs and bandage wounds. By the time we were finished, we knew the difference between flesh wounds and sucking chest wounds, what bandages to use, etc. Also, we were shown how to move patients, to get them in and out of bed safely. Practicing on oranges, we learned how to give injections. Of course, we also received instruction on positioning bed pans and how to remove and empty them. We spent countless hours receiving medical training so that we could work in a hospital setting.

Had we been preparing to go to work in military hospitals, the training we received would have been great. The military must have known that we were involved in an escalating conflict and that many combat medics would be required in Vietnam to treat wounds. What we really needed to learn was how to treat battle casualties and extreme injuries. In my opinion, we were very poorly trained in these areas. As I said, those in charge had to have known what the needs would be. One would have thought they would train us to fill these needs. Like many other things in the Army, this may have been by design.

Our training also included watching censored WWII movies. I guess they had us do this so that we would have an idea as to what things would be like in a combat setting. But these films were hard to relate to because they were very dated. Also, we were never shown what real battle wounds looked like. In retrospect, I think they purposely avoided showing us the real thing. They may have feared the wash-out rate that likely would have occurred. I know if I had seen in Advanced Individual Training (AIT) what I actually experienced in Vietnam, I would have tried to find a way to change my specialty. I'm sure a lot of other guys would have done so as well.

During my time in AIT, the Army switched from the M-14 rifle to the M-16, so we were introduced to the M-16 during one day of our medical training. In the morning we were given a lecture about the technical aspects of the weapon and its specifications. Each of us was given a rifle so that we could follow along with the instructions. With an empty magazine, we learned how to take the weapon apart, clean it, reassemble and load and unload it. In the afternoon, we went to a rifle range miles away from the base. There we were given eighteen rounds (bullets) to put in one magazine.

On the range, we were told to load the magazine and squeeze the rounds off at the target one by one. As a hospital corpsman, I couldn't figure out what the hell I was doing with this M-16.

So instead of putting the gauge in the single-shot position, I put it on automatic and sprayed the eighteen bullets in one burst. That was the extent of my rifle training as well as the end of any other weapons' training.

After hours, we had more freedom to do things than we had in basic training. I got involved in an evening flag football league. We played a couple of nights a week, and I enjoyed it. As wide receiver, I caught a lot of passes for the team. It was a great way to fill my evenings. Before I knew it I was starting to assimilate into the Army. I convinced myself that, if given the opportunity, I would have accepted an extended assignment at Ft. Sam Houston. It felt natural to be there. If a guy had to be in the Army, I thought to myself, being at a post that many considered the "country club" of the Army wasn't a bad thing.

In December 1967, near the end of my AIT, I heard rumors that our commanding officer had seen our orders for the next assignment and that many of the orders were very good. Obviously, we took "very good" to mean most of us were not going to Vietnam. That reassurance made us feel somewhat relaxed during our last few weeks of training. In fact, it almost lulled us to sleep on the issue. We wanted to think we wouldn't be going to Vietnam. The truth is, we needed to think we weren't going to Vietnam. The closer we got to the end of our training, the more fearful we were of going there. We were just a few weeks away from learning our futures.

Our training progressed and soon we were facing the end of this cycle. I thought I had learned enough to be a very capable hospital corpsman. I could give shots and readily locate veins for transfusions. Also, I was good at suturing. I was quick at identifying instruments and getting them into the trainer's hands quickly. I could set broken limbs, safely move patients as needed to prevent bed sores. There was no question in my mind that I was ready for a hospital assignment. What I had not been trained for was being a combat medic. That position required a different skill set, a different attitude and much different training than I had received.

Orders for Overseas Assignment

O N THE LAST DAY OF OUR advanced individual training we were all assembled out back on the football field. The commanding officer started reading off our orders. It's important to note that to be sent to a war zone, one had to be at least eighteen years old. We had some trainees who were still seventeen. They could receive overseas assignments like Germany, but not Vietnam. Members of the National Guard and Army Reserves who were training with us would also not receive overseas assignments.

The captain started in alphabetical order: Anderson—Vietnam; Arby—Vietnam; Artrip— Vietnam; Arturo—Vietnam and so forth. At this point, I just knew the "good orders" labeled so by our commanding officer were really good for shit and that we were probably all headed to Vietnam. As the captain got closer to my name, I had this sick feeling that I was going to Vietnam. I didn't have to wait long to hear it: Purtell—Vietnam. I realized then and there that I was going to get what I asked for six months earlier in a macho discussion with my high school friends. The guy who thought he was so tough was going to Vietnam.

Standing there feeling suddenly alone with the knowledge that I'd be in a country 14,000 miles away where a war was raging, believe me, I did not feel one bit tough or macho. I felt very demoralized. The captain rolled through the rest of the orders. I was too stunned to remember much more. We were told that evening that we would find out the next day where in Vietnam we'd be assigned, and the unit would also be identified. So I went to bed that night not knowing where in Vietnam I was going nor to what unit I'd be attached. I only knew I was definitely going to Vietnam. I slept very little that night.

The next morning, on or around January 12, 1968, I learned that I had been assigned to an engineering outfit in Cam Rahn Bay, Vietnam. I was told by people more knowledgeable than myself that I was leaving Ft. Sam Houston, the "country club" in the United States and going to the "country club" in Vietnam called Cam Rahn Bay. To be going there, I was told, meant that I would not likely be involved in any hostile action as the engineers had built roads in a very safe area in Vietnam. I was assured that, for someone going to Vietnam, I had received excellent orders. After hearing these positive reports about where I was going, I began to feel better about my assignment.

On Leave
Before Vietnam

I T WAS A GENERAL PRACTICE THAT AFTER a soldier received orders for Vietnam, he would get thirty days leave. I was scheduled to arrive at Cam Rahn Bay at the 18th Engineering Brigade on February 17, 1968. Before my departure, I returned to my home in Oshkosh, Wisconsin, to enjoy the little time I had left. When I got there, I first told my girlfriend Donna and then my buddies and family that I'd be going to Vietnam. The mood was very somber. I tried to lighten things up by telling them that I was going to a very safe area and that there was really nothing to worry about. Each morning that I woke up in Oshkosh, I knew it was one less day I had left to live in this country. As one might expect, I spent a lot of time with family, friends and with Donna. The thirty days were speeding by.

While I was home, I watched the television reports about Vietnam with much greater interest than ever before. In January 1968, the U.S. was introduced to the Tet Offensive. According to the media, this was a great Communist military victory because the enemy demonstrated that they could hit many different cities and outposts at the same time, something they had not done before. I could see that there was a subtle shift going on with the media and the situation in Vietnam. Soon after Tet, members of the media began asking, seemingly for the first time, whether we as a country were doing the right thing in Vietnam. As I was listening to the news reports and the commentary, I thought to myself, "Within days, I'll be there!"

Leaving Home

On February 13, 1968, I was driven to Oshkosh Whitman Field airport. I stood there with my parents and Donna awaiting the flight that would take me first to Chicago and then to Seattle, to Ft. Lewis, which was the departure point for Vietnam. For several moments, we only made small talk as this was very uncomfortable for everyone. We saw the plane come in. After it was refueled, it was ready for boarding. Saying goodbye, I hugged my mother and shook my father's hand and walked the short distance to the gate with Donna. When we stopped, I brought her to me, held her tight and kissed her. I told her not to worry because I would make it back.

It was below freezing when I walked outside the terminal to the twin engine plane. As it took off from the snow-covered runway, I didn't look back to try to see Donna or my parents. I knew I was screwed. I knew I was heading to a bad place. It was good they weren't able see me tear up. I knew I had volunteered for this. Yet, as we flew farther away from Oshkosh, alone with my thoughts, I began to wonder how I could ever measure up as a man and a soldier. Before long, we landed in Chicago, and I got on a flight headed for Ft. Lewis, Washington.

PART TWO

On My Way
to Vietnam

B ECAUSE I WAS THERE FOR ONLY A FEW DAYS, my recollection
of Ft. Lewis is not very clear. I do remember that I hooked
up with some other soldiers headed to Vietnam, and we drank a
lot of beer in the evenings and speculated about what we'd be
facing. Rudy Cardin, who was originally from Marinette, WI,
and who trained with me as a medic at Ft. Sam Houston, was one
of my drinking buddies for our short stint at Ft. Lewis, WA. Rudy
went on to serve as a combat medic with the 196th Infantry near
Chu Lai, Vietnam. I recall, too, that we had to sign a lot of forms,
probably the Army's version of a last will, insurance, etc. And
before we could go overseas, we had to get our injections. We
weren't assigned any duties other than cleaning up the grounds.
Ft. Lewis was just a stopover that ended too quickly.

On February 16, 1968, I boarded a Braniff flight, our final
destination being Cam Rahn Bay, Vietnam. We stopped for fuel
in Hawaii, Wake Island and the Philippine Islands. We were
allowed to deplane for a short time in a few locations, including
Hawaii. It was a very long flight. I remember feeling afraid and
alone. I must have spoken with other people, but I have no
recollection of any conversations. Here I was a few weeks shy of
my nineteenth birthday, and I'd never felt so cut off from others.

There was no one to show me the ropes or to tell me what to expect.

Though there were others around me, I felt completely alone in that plane headed for Vietnam, and I was afraid.

When we were approaching Vietnam, I could see the China Sea below and the land formation.

My fear was still with me. The first thing I thought of was whether bullets would, or could be, fired at our plane. Fortunately, they weren't, and we landed safely. When I got off the plane, the heat and humidity hit me like a ton of bricks. The temperature was around ninety-six degrees, and the humidity had to be around ninety percent. I also noticed that the place had a distinctly different smell. I was definitely in a foreign country. All of us had on our dress khakis which became very uncomfortable in that extreme heat, but no one complained. After all, we had just landed in Vietnam, and everyone was preoccupied with quietly processing the new information and mentally feeling our own way.

Once our luggage had been cleared, we grabbed our heavy duffel bags and began the long walk to the bus. It dawned on me right then that a few days earlier I had been in icy Wisconsin, and now I was in the tropical zone of Vietnam. The contrast was incredible to me, but there wasn't a lot of time to think about it. I got on the bus and waited to be taken to my new engineering outfit.

Whenever you arrive in a new area, you take care to check out your surroundings. Believe me, you're even more careful when you find yourself in a war zone. I was looking at everything, taking it all in. The bus finally took off down a red sandy road and delivered me safely to my next assignment, the base where I would get processed in.

Cam Rahn Bay

SOON I FOUND MYSELF IN CAM RAHN BAY, where I reported to the 18th Engineering Brigade office. After identifying myself, I was processed in and shown my room where I moved and unpacked my belongings. Then I was introduced to the person who would be my supervisor and proceeded to get acquainted with my surroundings. To my surprise, I was actually impressed with the facility. It was beautiful! Already, I was starting to get comfortable in my new environment. I was feeling pretty lucky to have been assigned to this very modern base and was anxious to get started at the medical clinic. As I looked around at the people, I realized that none of them showed any fear. What a cozy assignment, I thought to myself. It seemed that what I had heard was true: Cam Rahn Bay was the "country club" of Vietnam. I was really looking forward to spending my year there with the 18th Engineering Brigade in Cam Rahn Bay.

I had free time in the evenings, so I wrote to Donna and my parents telling them what a great place I'd been assigned to. I told them not to worry because I was in a very safe and secure place. Then, on my third day at Cam Rahn Bay, I was talking with two other medics when my supervising sergeant came up to us and told us to gather our stuff and report to the helicopter pad. Assuming we were going on a medical field trip, I asked him what he wanted us to gather. He said, "Get all of your personal belongings together. You guys have been reassigned." Thinking he'd made a mistake, I said, "You don't understand. I have orders to be a medic with the 18th Engineers here in Cam Rahn Bay." He said to me, "Soldier, your orders have been changed. Now get your shit together and report to the helicopter pad immediately. There's been a lot of action up north and they need medics up there now."

Not having a clue as to what had just happened to me, I scrambled back to my room. I'd no sooner gotten comfortable in my new surroundings than I was being rushed to a different area in Vietnam. Not only that, but given what the sergeant said, I'd be going to a hostile area. Having prepared myself mentally for the safety of Cam Rahn Bay, I wasn't even close to being ready for such a big change. It was particularly hard because it was sprung on me without any warning whatsoever. But what could I do? I was in the Army. I had no choice but to follow orders, so I quickly threw my stuff back in my duffel bag and reported to the helicopter pad.

Within minutes the helicopter arrived and, with long faces, we all got on. As the chopper departed, I looked down and watched Cam Rahn Bay disappear from view. There was no way I could communicate to my family that I was no longer in the place where they thought I was. I'd have to write to them once I got where we were going, wherever that was. I asked one of the people on board exactly where we were headed. He said we were going north to Chu Lai. Apparently, there had been a lot of enemy action in the north, so infantry units were in immediate need of medics. When I learned that I'd be assigned to an infantry unit, I couldn't believe it. This was the absolute worst news I could have possibly gotten. I thought I'd be in Cam Rahn Bay for my entire tour, so I hadn't really studied a map of Vietnam. I had no idea where Chu Lai was.

I was getting more fearful and apprehensive by the minute, in part because I didn't feel qualified to be a combat medic. Although I was confident that I'd be a good hospital corpsman, I never felt that I was properly trained at Ft. Sam Houston to handle gunshot or mortar wounds. I had no confidence at all in my ability to handle these new responsibilities. It's no wonder I was scared.

Chu Lai

WE LANDED IN CHU LAI IN I CORPS, which was very different from Cam Rahn Bay. Chu Lai looked and even smelled like a third-world country. Imagine human sweat from the tropical heat combined with the rotting jungle and fumes from diesel fuel. That's what surrounded me as I rode by jeep on dusty red roads to a processing point where I was to attend an in-country training program before being assigned to the next unit. Unlike previous training we'd gone through, in-country training was geared toward teaching us how to survive in Vietnam. This training was very beneficial. We were taught by experienced people who had been in the country for awhile. They gave us a pretty good sense of what we could come to expect for the next year.

After a few days of Vietnam orientation, I found out that I'd been assigned to Headquarters Company 1/6th 198th Light Infantry Brigade. I was transported to LZ (landing zone) Bayonet. Compared to Cam Rahn Bay, this base was relatively small. There were tents everywhere. I had left what felt to me like modern civilization at my former post, and now I was in an outpost surrounded by sand-bagged bunkers and barbed wire. What made it all harder to comprehend was that this drastic change happened in a very short period of time.

Soon I was introduced to some other medics awaiting assignment and to Sergeant Webb who would be my supervisor.

One of the first things I noticed was that, in a military sense and in attitude, this base camp was much more informal. Also, the lines between enlisted men and officers were, I thought, drastically blurred.

Sergeant Webb welcomed me to Headquarters Company. He told me that the following day I would be sent out to the field to join up with Charlie Co. 1/6th 198th Infantry. When I lay down on my cot that evening, I realized that I had no idea what was to come. I was so scared and anxious that I barely slept at all. Once again, what was preying on my mind was the fact that I had not been trained for this shit.

The following day I was issued an M-16 and ammunition. When I had the thing in my hands, I realized that I should have taken the M-16 training more seriously during AIT. But at that time, I didn't think I'd need it. Obviously, I was wrong. This was truly the real deal.

Sergeant Webb showed me how to pack a medical bag and ruck sack efficiently. I soon learned that a ruck sack basically held everything you needed to live out in the jungle. On the sergeant's advice, I packed two pairs of socks, some C-rations, writing paper and envelopes, mosquito repellant, ammunition for the M-16, another set of fatigues, a towel, razor, etc. As if the ruck sack wasn't heavy enough when I put it on, Sergeant Webb added to the weight by attaching a portable shovel called an entrenching tool. With the M-16 and the medical bag, I probably had between sixty and eighty pounds that I'd be carrying wherever I went. Even though I was in good shape, I began to doubt that I could carry all this weight for a long distance. It felt heavy and bulky on my back.

Soon I would find out if I could manage it all.

More bulky than heavy, the medical bag held bandages, various ointments, medical tape, scissors, morphine syringes, pills to prevent malaria and other medical-related supplies. Since the morphine was a narcotic, I had to sign a slip saying that I had been issued four syringes and that I would suffer a penalty should I not account for them properly. Though the bag itself wasn't heavy, I was beginning to realize that my responsibilities were.

But I resigned myself to my fate, thinking I was as ready as I was ever going to be to go out into the field. Since there was nothing honorable I could do about it, I accepted this big and unexpected change in my situation. No one I knew ever refused an assignment out in the field. At the time, I'd been told that refusal would have resulted in severe discipline and possibly jail. So, whether I wanted to or not, off I went.

Sergeant Webb shook my hand, wished me good luck and told me to go to the helicopter pad. I was to join Charlie Company out on an operation somewhere west of Chu Lai. He told me that, after I spent six months out in the field, I would be rotated back to LZ (Landing Zone) Bayonet. Medics, he said, were required to spend at least six months in the field.

To the Jungle

WITH MY RUCK SACK AND MEDICAL BAG on and my M-16 over my shoulder, I made my way to the helicopter pad where two other guys were waiting. From our quick little chat, I learned that these guys would not be accompanying me on the first chopper. So, I sat down away from them and waited.

Before long, I heard the sound that would stay with me forever: the wop, wop, wop sound of rotating helicopter blades. As the chopper approached the pad, I heard a loud explosion. I instinctively rolled to find cover. I had no idea what had happened, but I knew it wasn't good. One of the guys who had been at the pad with me was holding a mutilated, bloody hand and was screaming "Medic!" This was the first time I heard the word "medic" from someone who was actually in pain. (I learned later that the guy had some blasting caps in his pack which may have been set off by the rotating blades and caused the injury). I immediately ran over to the wounded soldier to render aid. At about the same time, Sergeant Webb appeared and told me he would handle it. He gestured me to board the helicopter that had just landed. So I moved towards the chopper door.

Quickly, I got on the chopper. There were only four other guys on board including the pilot, co-pilot and two door gunners. Because of the explosion, I was already flustered. I was trying to process what had just happened. Also, having seen all that blood for the first time, I was a bit sickened. At Ft. Sam Houston, they never showed us the blood. Some people get sick at the sight of blood while others faint. Though I didn't faint, I did get a sick feeling in my stomach. On that day, I learned that blood has a very distinctive smell, particularly when it's mixed with gun powder. It's a smell that stays with you long after you've left the area.

I was on the chopper alone for about twenty minutes. Even if someone had been available, I would not have been able to have a conversation because of the noise. Equipped with a machine gun mounted to the helicopter, the door gunners had their fingers on their triggers as they gazed below. The pilot and co-pilot were focused on flying the helicopter. Here I was getting ready to go out on my first day with an infantry company where I wouldn't know a soul and, in my first ten minutes, I had already experienced an explosion and seen a bloody wound. It didn't look as if things were going to get any better out in some damn jungle. I began to wonder how I could ever come out of this alive.

When our helicopter started moving in for a landing, I saw yellow smoke and had no idea what it was for. While I was in the chopper, no one had prepped me regarding what to expect. Nor was I told how the chopper would land and what I was to do when it did land. In other words, I didn't know the protocol. Apparently, no one had thought about that. I had not received infantry training. I was a medic, for God's sake. My job, as I understood it, was to be moving patients around in some cozy hospital setting. Instead, I was headed down near some damn smoke. I couldn't see a living person down below. All I could see was the green of the jungle and yellow smoke.

The chopper touched down and the door gunner yelled, "Get out!" I yelled back: "There's nobody here." He grabbed my arm and shouted again: "Get out!" Against my better judgment, I quickly got off the chopper and immediately it rose from the makeshift landing and was whisked away. I was standing alone within the glow of the yellow smoke. No one else was in sight. I thought I was really fucked. I didn't know what the hell was going on. Why was the Army doing this to me? At the time, I didn't know what panic attacks were; but I can assure you I was not doing well on the inside. Seconds later, from behind the foliage, I started making out images of American soldiers. What a welcome sight! I felt instant relief. My heart moved from my throat back to my chest. I wanted to go home.

Welcome to the War

O F COURSE, I KNEW I WASN'T GOING HOME, so I began to settle
in as best I could. The first guy I met on the ground was Al
Torsiello from Union, New Jersey. Like myself, he was a newer
guy too, having arrived a few weeks earlier in February 1968.
One of the first questions he asked was where I was from.
"Oshkosh, Wisconsin," I said. Rather excitedly he replied, "No
shit? Prove it!"

I wasn't sure what I was supposed to prove, but I went along
with the drill and pulled out my wallet and showed him an old
ID card. Al yelled to another guy, "Bean, there really is an
Oshkosh." Then he explained to me that for people living on the
east coast in the U.S., Oshkosh was a mythical place. When they
thought someone was full of shit or telling tall stories, they'd tell
the culprit: "Go to Oshkosh." This was news to me. I'd never
thought about how outsiders viewed my home town.

The guy Al yelled to was Gene Lynch from Brooklyn, New
York. Everyone called him Bean. He was a very muscular guy,
Irish, with red hair and freckles, a really smooth character. I could
tell right away that I had just met someone unlike anyone I'd ever
met. He was a guy who exuded personality, and it was clear that
Al respected him. Welcoming me to the second platoon, Bean
said, "Hi, Doc." No one had every called me "Doc" before, so I
wasn't prepared for it. I was no longer Jim Purtell. For as long as

I'd be with these guys, and it was a long time, I was known as Doc. It made me feel kind of special. Foolish me! I didn't know at the time that all the medics in Vietnam were called Doc. Once again, no one told me.

Bean did make it a point to tell me that I had some big shoes to fill. Their former medic, Pratt, had been killed in a terrible fight a few weeks before. Bean spoke of him with great reverence as he described the former medic's heroism. I'll never forget how I felt listening to Bean talk about Pratt. It was almost a religious experience because it resonated with me that I had a far bigger job in front of me than I had ever realized. The feelings of self-doubt came back to me in a more pronounced way: How would I ever measure up to everybody's expectations?

I was soon introduced to others in the platoon, Lieutenant Ernie Carrier and Staff Sergeant Leroy Ferguson, among others. Sergeant Ferguson let me know that I'd be under his supervision. He said that, once we started moving, I would be in a small unit with a radio operator named Pye and Lt. Carrier. Sergeant Ferguson said I was to stay glued to Lt. Carrier at all times.

It was obvious that Sgt. Ferguson took the Army spit-and-polish very seriously, as he always appeared freshly groomed. I don't know how he did it. He was a staff sergeant, and there weren't many in his rank out in the field. At the time, I didn't know why that was the case. I do know that Ferguson rubbed some guys the wrong way. Guys in the infantry didn't see any reason to put up with the bullshit that goes along with appearance. There were more important things to do, like try to stay alive. Career soldiers like Ferguson thought things should be done a certain way, and some of the infantry guys just didn't agree.

It was soon clear to me that the platoon was very happy to have a medic with them. I didn't understand at that time that, to an infantryman, the most important person, if he got hit by any projectile, was the medic. If they were wounded, they didn't trust another infantryman to help them, only the medic. They wanted someone who'd been trained in the medical field. Also, it's important to remember that these guys had been without a medic for a few weeks now, and that made them extremely nervous. If they had known the extent of my combat medical training, which was almost nil, they would have been terrified.

Al said he'd introduce me to the others guys. We went around, and I met each guy in the platoon, approximately thirty altogether. Though I'm sure I knew their first names at that time, everyone out in the jungle, or bush or boonies, as it was called in our unit, was referred to by last name. Al told me how important it was to watch what the older guys did once "the shit hit the fan." As he put it, "Watch them closely and do what they do." When I looked around, I asked, "Who are the older guys?" To me, they all looked to be close to my age or a few years older, and I was about to turn nineteen. Al then explained that the unit I had just joined came from an Army base in Texas. Several of these guys had trained together in the States and then came to Vietnam by boat in October 1967. Some of them had been together a long time, so they were a tight unit. Pointing to them, Al rattled off their names: Bean, Louie Panteleon, Eddie McCracken, Gypsy, Daryl Herlocker, Scott and Provost. These were some of the older guys. He repeated: "Watch these guys."

The second platoon was one of three infantry platoons in Charlie Company. I discovered that we had first and third platoons as well as a mortar platoon which rarely operated out in the field. Typically, the mortar platoon would be situated on some protected hill or base, and they would provide fire support whenever it was called in by military commanders. Each platoon had roughly thirty guys, so our company was about ninety strong or 120 if you counted the mortar platoon. The structure within the platoon was typically a second lieutenant, a senior non-commissioned officer, a medic, a radio operator and twenty-six riflemen.

The next person I met was Captain Hurtado who welcomed me to Charlie Company. He was the highest ranking officer out in the field, the guy who made the command decisions on the ground. He had the senior medic travel with him. The reason for this was so that, if he were to be hit by gunfire or shrapnel, a medic would be close by to provide assistance as quickly as possible. Statistics show that the sooner someone received medical attention, the higher the rate of survival. Since the officer was the most important person in the command structure, it was important for the group that he be kept as safe as possible.

As I was continuing to take everything in, I looked around at the other guys and was surprised by their lack of hygiene and their slovenly personal appearance, something I wasn't used to.

Their boots were worn, scuffed and reddish brown, much like the color of the red sandy roads. My boots, in contrast, were spit-shined black. Their hair was much longer than the military considered appropriate, while mine was short and neatly trimmed. Their fatigues were ill-fitted, while mine had nice lines. It didn't take long to figure out that none of that spit-shine and discipline, which was so important in basic training and AIT, mattered in the least out in the bush. I would have to readjust and forget what was stressed in my earlier training. It wasn't important. I was now out in the jungle with many battle-hardened veterans whose only concern was staying alive so they could get back home.

Everyone was eager to hear news from home. Since there were no phones, televisions or newspapers out in the jungle, their only sources of new information were from guys like me, who had just joined them, or letters that often took weeks to arrive. I brought them up to speed on the political situation in the States and what songs and bands were popular. I also let them know about the seemingly shifting view of the war among Americans. They listened with great interest. It's as if hearing about what was going on in the States made them feel less cut off from home.

I liked Al Torsiello right away, and I trusted him. To get a feel for how to act out in the jungle, I decided to stick close to him. I watched closely as he prepared his food, and I did it the same way. We were all issued a P-38 which was a very small metal device that served as a can opener. Al and the other guys opened the C-ration cans from the top about two-thirds of the way around the top of the can and then bent the top back so it formed a handle. Then they would heat whatever was in the container (spaghetti and meatballs, chunky chicken, beans and franks, chopped beef or ham and lima beans, more popularly referred to as ham and motherfuckers) using heat tablets on the ground or on a rock or in an empty can. The Army provided the heat tablets. Occasionally, when they'd get resupplied, guys would cook with C4, an explosive ingredient. They'd strike a match and ignite the heat tablet or C-4 and cook whatever they chose to eat on a given day. Once the necessary holes were punched in the sides of the cans so the heat would flow evenly, some guys got creative and used some of their smaller empty cracker or cookie cans as stoves. Some would heat up cheese and fry a piece of ham and put it between crackers. All of these food products came in separate cans, so it required an effort and some ingenuity. Paying close attention to Al, I learned pretty quickly how to manage all of these clever tricks for preparing food out in the jungle.

My first afternoon out there was coming to a close. I was briefed on how we as a platoon would set up our perimeter and who would be positioned where. We were told who would be on guard duty and who would be responsible for setting out claymore mines outside our perimeter. Al was the guy who coached me through these things. The infantry guys already knew how to do all of this because they'd gone through infantry training and jungle school for months. I, on the other hand, had been trained to empty bed pans. I was reminded once again how ill prepared I was for the situation I found myself in.

Incoming

D ARKNESS CAME AND IT WAS QUIET IN OUR CAMP. Out in the field, when it got dark, all cigarettes went out, and we observed silence. Those who were on guard duty went into position, while the rest of us retired to sleeping areas on the ponchos we'd placed on the ground. It wasn't long after dark when the solitude was interrupted by a mortar attack. If you listened closely, you could distinctly hear off in the distance the sound of the canister round going down the enemy's mortar tube followed by a whirling sound as the round traveled towards us rotating at a high rate of speed through the air.

I heard some of our guys yell, "Incoming"! At the time it didn't mean anything to me. I quickly learned that it was a warning from fellow soldiers that enemy mortar rounds would soon be coming upon us. The next sound was a thud, which was the sound the round made when it first hit the solid ground. Then you heard an explosion that sent shrapnel in virtually all directions. Al whispered so I could hear: "Doc, we're getting mortared." "What do I do?" I asked. He told me to stay right where I was. "They usually walk the rounds in," he said, "so you have a better idea after the second one explodes where they're going to be and where you should be." Another round came in closer to where we were, followed by a third and fourth round, and that was it.

Just like that it was over. Fortunately, no one was injured in this short mortar attack. On my first night in the jungle, it seemed as if I'd taken a crash course, Introduction to War 101. Not having been trained in advance, I was learning on the job, so to speak. I felt I had been baptized, in a different sort of way, by the incoming rounds. It was a very scary experience. I knew then that this would be a long year.

The Morning After
and Resupplies

THE NEXT MORNING, WE GOT UP, prepared coffee over our hastily made stoves. We sat around smoking cigarettes and talking about the mortar attack. These guys had already undergone several mortar attacks and found them to be the most terrifying experiences of the war. One of the reasons for this is that they could hear the mortars coming in, but they never knew where the first one was going to land. It was that uncertainty, plus the damage that they could inflict, that made the vets fearful.

During the day time, the guys were constantly smoking. I was no exception. As I recall, very few of the guys didn't smoke. In fact, the Army furnished us with cigarettes when they brought in C-rations, clean uniforms, mail and water by helicopter. Guys would argue over which brand of cigarettes they would get. Some, like myself, liked Marlboros; some wanted Salems or Kools or Camels. They were also picky about C-rations. The ham and motherfucker (lima bean) meal was the one most scorned. Often, the last guy in line would get that meal and would piss and moan about getting stuck with it. Occasionally, you'd find a guy who liked the ham and lima beans.

When you found that guy, you constantly supplied him if you got stuck with it. There was a lot of horse trading for meals, whether it be turkey loaf or beef slices, spaghetti and meat balls or beans and franks. Everyone seemed to find a way to get the food they could tolerate.

Clean uniforms would come in old mail bags, and guys would run to these bags, grab a pair of fatigues and quickly try them on. If they were even close to your size, meaning they fit you around the waist and you got your upper body in the shirt portion, you'd keep them. Even if they were sometimes ill-fitting, they were at least clean; and that's all that mattered. It wasn't unusual to wear the same pair of fatigues for a month.

Pissing and Moaning

A FEW DAYS EARLIER, I HAD BEEN IN a training environment where we adhered strictly to military order, which meant we'd answer with "yes sir" and "no sir" and "yes ma'am." But out in the field, I learned very early on that guys would piss and moan about everything. Initially, I didn't understand this. After all, I'd just completed four and a half months of military training and any complaining that went on was minimal. Here, though, it was just the opposite. Although I could have pissed and moaned about my inadequate medical training, I didn't want to mention that in front of guys who would be depending on me to use the skills that they thought I had. Or, I could have bitched about getting plucked from a cozy environment and reassigned with these infantry guys, but I didn't want to do that either. What I did instead was simply listen to what they said and respond by saying, "God damn it! You're right!"

It didn't take long to join in the chorus. We'd complain about the Army, the fact that some guys had been drafted. Or they'd get off on guys who'd joined. When they found out that I was an enlistee and the son of a dentist, they wondered how I had fucked up so badly and got stuck out there with them. They would ride my ass, though in a good-natured way. Guys would also piss and moan about having been sent to infantry school and winding up in Vietnam. We'd complain about the weather, the mosquitoes, the leeches, the food. Everything was game, the leaders we had, the areas we had to cover, how far we had to hump (walk). Virtually every other subject known to man was something to bitch about. The only thing that stopped this pissing and moaning, as we were humping, was getting shot at or mortared. Darkness would halt the complaining too. Because we were a miserable lot stuck in a miserable place, the rest of our waking hours were spent crabbing about just about everything.

Boredom

ONE WOULD THINK THAT GUYS IN VIETNAM would not get bored. But that was not the case. Each day we would start off the same way, and we'd always have orders to hump a certain number of klicks. Each klick represented 1,000 meters. We would load up our ruck sacks, move away from our former perimeter area and begin our hump. Guys would be put out on flank, and we'd start walking to our night position. All along the way, we'd be talking about how hot it was, about somebody's girlfriend, our favorite song or what we were going to do when we got home. Each of us had our back-in-the-world stories that we'd relay to each other. Sometimes, in the early days, we would have no action at all. During those times, we'd forget we were even in a war.

When nothing was happening, it wasn't unusual to get lulled to sleep. Then, all of a sudden, something bad would happen, and we'd realize, once again, what we were doing there.

Lieutenant Carrier

L IEUTENANT CARRIER WAS THE GUY WHO issued orders to us in the second platoon. He'd constantly remind me: "Doc, make sure the guys get all of their malaria pills." Because mosquitoes in Vietnam carried malaria, each soldier had to take a daily white anti-malaria pill and a weekly brown pill. It was my responsibility to see that the guys took these pills. I must have been doing my job right because, to my knowledge, no one in my platoon got malaria. Lieutenant Carrier was on top of things too, making sure I was doing what I was supposed to do for the guys.

Carrier was a very aggressive guy. Some people liked him and others didn't. My friend Al didn't like him, but I did. Carrier, who was from Louisiana, was a bit cocky, I'll admit. But to me, he demonstrated confidence, which I translated as leadership. I almost never saw him flustered. His orders were decisive. I admired him so much, in fact, that I went where he went. Despite my close access to him, though, I was not privy to where we would conduct our operations. In the early days, Carrier got his general operating instructions from Captain Hurtado, person to person, along with the lieutenants from the first and third platoons. Then, Carrier would brief the platoon sergeants and squad leaders who would then brief their squads. Lieutenant Carrier was so effective that, as far as I know, none of our platoon members were killed while he led us.

Scrutinizing the Medic

VERY EARLY ON, I SENSED THAT SOME of the guys were watching me, trying to gauge what kind of medic I would be. It's not that anyone said anything to me directly. It was more of a gut feeling, a vibe I picked up on. Of course, it was understandable that they'd wonder about me. Their lives were at stake, after all. Not only that but, just a few weeks earlier, they'd lost their favorite medic in a battle; and that loss was fresh in their minds. They spoke about Pratt, their former aid man, with a kind of reverence. I, on the other hand, was an unknown commodity, so they were unsure about me. I had not yet been tested, and I'm certain they wondered what kind of medic I would be under fire. I sensed their lack of trust, and it was pretty unsettling.

Though I don't think I showed a lack of self-confidence in front of these guys, I knew, deep down, that I had not been trained for this shit. In fact, as I saw it, in 1967-68 (compared to, for example, a Navy corpsman), none of the Army medics received training sufficient to handle the wounds we would encounter. So it was understandable that I would have feelings of self-doubt about my ability to be as effective as the medics who'd had the right training.

Clearing the Roads

I N THE BEGINNING OF MY VIETNAM JUNGLE TOUR, our mission was to patrol the roads from LZ Baldy to LZ Ross. The Viet Cong often placed mines or booby traps in the dirt road and nearby areas. Our role was to walk behind engineers and scour the areas in front, to the sides and to the rear to provide protection for them as they swept the roads using bomb detectors. When they found what they believed to be bombs, they motioned to us and we were ordered to stop in place. Then the engineers would have us back up, and they would either skillfully disarm the bomb; or if they felt uncomfortable about a particular bomb, they would clear us out of the area while they blew it up. Finishing a stretch of road would allow for the safe transport of men, supplies and materials to outlying locations. That was the purpose of the whole exercise.

When a road that was designated to be cleared was finished, we would often branch out in the surrounding areas on search-and-clear missions. These were designed to get a sense of who, in terms of the enemy, was operating in the immediate area. We wanted to make sure our surroundings were as safe as reasonably could be expected under the circumstances. So we would reconnoiter the area to see what we could find.

The first time I walked into a village in a rural area and entered a Vietnamese hooch (house), I was struck by the poverty before me. For the most part, the hooches I saw were very small and made of bamboo for the framing and thick wads of straw or grass for the roofs. They had dirt floors and no electricity or plumbing. Water was drawn at the community well. The bathroom seemed to be in an outlying area away from the hooch, anywhere the people wanted to do their business.

In these searches, we primarily encountered women and children and old men. They were often dressed in black garb. When we foolishly asked if they were Viet Cong, they would respond in what sounded like gibberish. Many of them wore conical hats, and they appeared to be afraid of us.

We would search the villages and look for evidence of any materials to support the war effort, be it ammunition, caches of weapons or large storage areas for food. Rarely did we find anything of value, nor did we find young men. We figured that the reason we didn't see any military-aged men was because they were Viet Cong.

In the early days, February or March 1968, we would occasionally receive sniper fire while out on search-and-clear missions. When we were fired upon, we returned fire. I'll never forget the first time I came upon a Vietnamese man who had been wounded in one of these engagements. He'd been shot through his right side. The entry hole was the size of a dime with the edges of the wound pointed in. When I examined him on the other side of his body, I found that the exit wound was about five times the size of the entry wound. The reason for this was because the ammunition we used would enter a body and start tumbling, causing large exit wounds. This also caused the edges of the wounds to point out. I could tell by the look on the man's face that he was in great pain; and, naturally, he was afraid of me. I gently applied bandages to both sides of the wounds and, when the helicopter arrived, I picked him up with my hands beneath his knees and his head and carried him to the chopper. After the chopper took off, some of the guys said, "What the fuck did you do that for?" I had no idea what they were talking about. Apparently, I was supposed to "just throw the gook [slang for Vietnamese] on the chopper without providing medical care to him and be done with it." I was taken aback by their comments and their tone. But I was new out in the bush, so I just let it go. Given my medical training and my own value system, I couldn't have done anything else but render aid.

Throughout February and March 1968, we continued to provide protection for the engineers who were clearing the roads (Hwy 1). As we did so, we searched nearby areas looking to encounter or draw out the enemy. We had occasional brief firefights, but most of our action occurred at night when we would get mortared. It seemed to me to be the kind of mortaring meant to harass us and let us know the enemy was out there. I don't recall many injuries from these mortar attacks early on. That did not make them any less stressful and scary.

Chieu Hoi and the
Hidden Hospital

I N MID- TO LATE-MARCH 1968, our mission changed. In our day-to-day dealings, we became more aggressive. We were definitely seeking out the enemy; but instead of search-and-clear missions, they were more oriented to search-and-destroy. On one of these searches, we were led by a North Vietnamese soldier who had defected under the recently implemented *Chieu Hoi* program. This program had been initiated a month earlier. Our government flew over North Vietnamese airspace and dropped propaganda pamphlets promising potential defectors that they would receive better treatment, have access to better food, clothing and weapons if they switched over to the U.S. side. I don't know how many North Vietnamese soldiers defected. The guy we had with us was the only one we knew. This young man who was now walking point (first in the formation, the most dangerous position) had been one of the Vietnamese who had responded to the program. He had apparently been vetted, or so we thought, and assigned to our unit for a short period of time.

On this particular day, Lieutenant Carrier briefed us that we would be on the lookout for a North Vietnamese hospital in the area. All that the intelligence personnel knew was that they had received information that the hospital was located somewhere in our area. As we were walking in this open area, we came upon a solitary hooch out in the middle of nowhere. Since this was unusual, we were, of course, suspicious. But, since no one spoke Vietnamese, other than the *Chieu Hoi*, we didn't know what to make of it. The *Chieu Hoi* went into the hooch, dragged out an elderly man and started angrily berating him and aggressively questioning him while we all watched. This was a first for us. When the *Chieu Hoi* didn't get the answers he was looking for, he started smacking the old man around and striking his face. This abuse went on for quite awhile. I couldn't figure out why this young man was beating the shit out of an old man?

Soon it became apparent why.

After taking quite a beating, the older Vietnamese man finally started giving up information. He nervously led the *Chieu Hoi* a few hundred yards to the edge of a heavily wooded area at the base of the mountain. We followed them and watched as the old man began selecting sheared branches that, to us, had perfectly blended into the landscape. He threw them aside. We were stunned to learn that we ourselves had not seen all of those branches, but they had been expertly camouflaged. Within minutes of removing several layers of green branches, the old man exposed a four to five foot wide stone staircase that had been carved into the mountain. We could not believe what we were seeing. We thought we'd hit the jackpot. Never had we seen anything like this in Vietnam. It had to have required a monumental effort to construct this stairway up the mountains right under the noses of the Americans. It was solid rock on all sides.

Lieutenant Carrier quickly told us what we were to do. The old Vietnamese guy was to be muzzled and guarded by a few of our troops. We were then to escalate up the stone steps but keep the proper distance, about ten feet between one another. As we whispered among ourselves, Sgt. Provost urged us not to open fire in this area as bullets could ricochet off of the very close mountainsides and come back and hit us. This would never have dawned on me, but Provost was well schooled in infantry training, a very smart and well respected guy.

As we made our way up the mountain, very carefully taking in everything, we reached a point where we could see the top of the stairs. We were stunned to see enemy weapons stacked upright vertically. I remembered having seen old photographs of the Civil War in which weapons were stacked in the same way. North Vietnamese guards dressed in khaki uniforms were asleep near the weapons. We were all blown away by this because we'd never before witnessed any lack of discipline in the enemy. But we rarely saw the enemy anyway, so we weren't sure whether or not we were being drawn into a trap.

Our guys, who were in front as they reached the top of the stairs, opened up with the M-16s on fully automatic and killed the North Vietnamese nearest the weapons. Then pandemonium broke out. These guys never knew what hit them. They likely woke for a few seconds and then they were dead. North Vietnamese soldiers (male and female) were running everywhere through the brush trying to escape as the rest of us made our way up the steps. Without a doubt, we had discovered the North Vietnamese hospital, and these people were doctors, nurses and other medical personnel along with armed guards.

We began shooting at anyone we saw wearing khaki-colored clothes. One North Vietnamese soldier, who we learned later was a doctor, tried to run through the brush; but it was so thick that there was no way out for him. He was shot in the head and killed. The enemy tried to escape in holes in the ground leading to tunnels, so we threw grenades down these holes. Altogether there were about twenty-four enemy soldiers killed. But because we totally surprised them and dispatched them quickly, we were not fired upon.

Shortly after this encounter, there was an explosion. Lieutenant Carrier yelled, "Doc, I'm hit." I raced to the area. He had come upon an enemy soldier who was lying face down on the ground pretending to be dead. But unbeknownst to Carrier, this guy had somehow pulled the pin on a grenade and blew himself up. Some of the enemy's bone had struck Carrier's ear. When I told him what I thought had happened, for a moment, he felt foolish; and we both laughed. Reflecting on this incident after the war, I wondered how we could find any humor in that situation. But I think the laughter was not the usual response that one would have to something funny but more of a necessary emotional relief.

Lieutenant Carrier radioed Captain Hurtado and briefed him about what we had discovered. The hospital was situated in the mountains, completely hidden from view from the ground and the air.

The only reason we were able to discover it was because we had a *Chieu Hoi* defector. Without him, we would have walked right by the well-camouflaged entrance. We probably weren't the only ones who failed to see what was there. No doubt several other Army units had walked past it many times without seeing it as well.

After things settled down, I walked around examining their medical facility. There was a wooden operating table with a shielded light up above powered by a very quiet generator. It was amazing to see how adaptable these third-world people were. After some time examining the facility, we quietly and somberly walked down the same stairs leaving the enemy where they fell. Reliving mentally what we had just done, I realized that if the North Vietnamese guards at the top of the steps had been alert instead of asleep at nine in the morning, they would have opened up their automatic weapons and we would have been in a terrible fix. We would have had to drag wounded people down the steps as quickly as possible to get them out of the line of fire and would surely have suffered numerous casualties in the process. Two or three napping guards caused their entire unit to be wiped out, and we never gave that incident another thought. We had just taken out a very strategic and important North Vietnamese hospital and had killed many valuable personnel, including, as we learned after the fact, a doctor and nurses. The medical outlet for the NVA (North Vietnamese Army) in that immediate area was now gone. We walked to the base of the stairs and back out into the grassy areas from which we had come. There was no time to dwell on what we'd just done. The war had to go on.

Because we rarely got to see the enemy and get that many kills, this had been a very unusual day. We referred to it as a "turkey shoot" because our firepower had been overwhelming and likely had been the only fire exchanged that day. In the midst of it all, we had killed many people who'd been doing a job similar to mine, so the incident was especially unnerving for me. Shortly afterwards, though, we saw bombs falling on the hospital compound to erase the medical facility that existed just hours before. So it was "mission accomplished," just another day in the life of an infantryman.

Digging and Pulling Guard Duty

A S WE DID EVERY NIGHT DURING THESE months of our tour of duty, we set up our night perimeter in an area nearby. With the entrenching tool that we carried on the back of our ruck sacks, we dug holes about ten feet apart. We dug them in such a way as to form a circle so that our platoon, depending on the operation we were conducting, could defend itself from any angle of attack. Digging foxholes at the end of the day after many klicks was not a pleasant task. Often, we would dig ten to twelve of them in many different kinds of terrain. I would dig mine deep and inward. I used to say that my foxholes were multi-leveled like two-story apartments. Sergeant Leroy Ferguson would joke with the guys, saying that I slept with one foot in the foxhole so that, at the first sound of the mortaring process, I was in the hole. A piece of shrapnel once hit against the edge of my hole, down about a foot, and fell harmlessly to the bottom. For awhile I wore that piece of shrapnel strapped to my helmet, but it got to feeling too heavy so I threw it away. If it had hit me, instead of the wall of my hole, it could have ripped off my arm, as it was that big and jagged.

When we stopped for the night, we always sought the highest ground in the area because it was easier to shoot down on the enemy and harder for the enemy to get up to us. We would dig in and then set out our claymore mines (rectangular cigar-box shaped mines that projected outwards, the wires connected to a detonator held by us in our fox holes) and then get ready for the evening. We'd open our C-rations, heat them, eat and then smoke cigarettes while pissing and moaning about anything until it got dark. When the smoking was done, silence was the order of the evening.

We'd then have guys who would stand guard, that is, be awake in their foxholes in two hour shifts watching for the enemy. I took my turn with great regularity. From the command post, we'd get radio calls, and our response was usually "Sitrep negative," which meant the situation report at that particular moment in that particular location was negative. Very often we would get two hours of sleep, pull guard duty, a little more sleep and then pull guard duty again. Continuous sleep through the night just didn't happen out in the field.

When I pulled guard, I would peer out in the darkness and look intently for any movement and sometimes imagine I saw something. Because I was fearful, I would be hyper alert. I didn't want to get killed or get any of our guys killed. It was a very scary and lonely existence. During those hours, I would yearn for family and friends and the safety of home. At the same time, I realized that I had a job to do and many more months to go to complete my year.

Even though I was a medic, by virtue of being with the infantry, I became an infantryman or a grunt, as they're called. The only way anyone could distinguish me from my buddy Al and the other infantry guys was by the unmarked medical bag I carried. There was no white cross on my bag or my helmet. Like the infantry guys, I had a ruck sack and an M-16. I also had a 38 pistol that I won in a poker game with some Vietnamese card players. In my filthy fatigues and brown boots, I looked just like the grunts. The new guys looked much different. You could always tell them from the base camp vets by the condition and fit of their fatigues, the black color of their boots and their clean-shaven look. We grunts developed a kind of attitude toward them, calling them newbies.

Among the infantry, I was known as hardcore and, for awhile, I myself thought I was hardcore. I had joined the Army because I was a tough guy. But, soon enough, the war brought me down and kicked the shit out of me.

Losing a Leader

ON APRIL 6, 1968, WE WERE ON A TYPICAL search-and-clear mission. Situated west of Chu Lai, we got the order to take five (a break). We brought out our canteens to take a drink, and I'm sure we lit up cigarettes and started bitching about something. Then suddenly one of three things happened. Either someone tripped on a wire, tugged on the wire, or it was hand-detonated by the enemy which caused a massive explosion. The bodies and body parts of Captain Hurtado and Dan Reid were blown everywhere. What could be found of them was gathered and put in body bags. A medevac helicopter was called in to evacuate them.

At that time, because we were engaging in squad and platoon activities apart from the other guys, we didn't know what had happened. So, one by one, we were instructed to evacuate the area and to, very carefully, watch our step. If we stepped on a mine (as we suspected we were in a mine field), we were to stand in place and not move a muscle. The first guy made it through unscathed, so we were told to try to walk exactly where the first guy had stepped. I gingerly stepped out of the area. I remember thinking that each step I took could be the last. In fact, I was expecting to feel the device on top of the mine or booby trap under my foot. Fortunately, it never happened. When we gathered again as a platoon, we speculated that it was one of the three scenarios described earlier that took Hurtado and Reid's lives. In seconds, they were gone from us, their loved ones and their friends forever.

For us guys in the infantry, to lose a captain was to lose the highest ranking guy we had out in the field. This was a very costly loss, as he was our top guy, the one the lieutenants went to for briefings and reports. He was the leader who called in gunships when needed or medevacs. Sure, there were higher ranking guys; but, except in very unusual circumstances, rarely did you see anybody out in the field higher in rank than a captain. I recall Colonel Kelly coming out in the field for a short time on a few occasions. But Captain Hurtado lived with us, slept among us, ate with us, humped with us and fought with us—and now he was gone. Needless to say, our morale began to suffer.

Two Months of Hell

ROM APRIL 6 UNTIL ABOUT JUNE 5, 1968, we were involved in a cycle of activity that had us in action seemingly every single day. During that time, either we were in a firefight, got ambushed or sniped at. Sometimes we lost guys due to booby traps. This period of heavier than normal action began to wear on us physically and psychologically. As a result, we grew angrier than ever at the unseen enemy.

Because Lt. Carrier took a staff position with MACV in Saigon near the end of April of 1968, he missed most of our combat experiences. His taking that position meant that we in the second platoon were not only without our top gun, Hurtado, but also without one of his top assistants, Ernie Carrier. Although another very able leader, Lt. Melvin Spencer (who may have taken command of a few platoons for a short time), took over the responsibility and assumed command of Charlie Company, it was still a very difficult time for us. We were losing buddies every day. Fortunately, many of those we lost were wounded and medevaced, and eventually found their way back to the U.S. with Purple Heart awards. Other guys rotated out, which meant they got to go home after they'd finished their twelve-month period of duty.

There were very few guys who were with the infantry for a year who made it through unwounded, though there were some.

So, with guys going home and guys getting killed and guys getting wounded on a regular basis, we'd get newbie replacements, and most of them had no idea what they were in for.

Hill 352

O<small>N</small> M<small>AY</small> 8, 1968, <small>WE WERE TOLD WE WERE</small> going to take this hill in the Central Highlands called Hill 352. The Second NVA Division was in the area, and we were in for some very heavy action. We made our way up the rugged hill a good distance when we located a plateau where we decided to establish a night position. Going up a hill with all of that weight on our backs was no easy task. Typically, there were no trails on the hills, so we put our feet where we thought we could get solid footing, grabbed at something overhead and kept moving up. Invariably, equipment would get stuck in brush or our ruck sacks would hook onto something.

It was never advantageous to be lower than the enemy, but this was a very difficult hill to climb. Also, it wasn't possible to continue moving up that late in the day. A small squad went out on a scouting mission and discovered some weaponry, which included a large-caliber machine gun. The members of the squad saw some enemy soldiers dressed in green uniforms watching them off in the distance. So we knew the enemy was nearby. The word quickly spread to everyone that the NVA were out there because the VC we had encountered did not wear green uniforms. We set up for the night, put out our protective claymore mines and followed our normal routine with guards and a tight perimeter. It was an eerie night. Knowing for sure we were among the enemy, we fully expected an attack at any point. But, as I recall, that did not happen.

However, my buddy Al remembers it differently. He thinks we got mortared that night. That certainly could have happened. Whether we were mortared or not, I will never forget how scary it felt to be hunkered down waiting through the night, thinking we'd be attacked at any moment by the NVA.

The next morning, we were told to drop our ruck sacks within our perimeter. Then we went outside and continued walking up Hill 352. My Staff Sergeant, Leroy Ferguson, 6'3" and about 225 pounds, the guy I reported to, asked, "Doc, do you have your morphine with you?" I had been out with him for three months, and this was the first time he asked me this question. To date, I had not had to administer morphine to anyone, so I said, "No." Sergeant Ferguson told me I'd best go back and get it. Obviously, he had a sense that it might be needed, so I did what I was ordered to do.

I rushed back to my rucksack, located the morphine syringes and threw them in my medical bag. Then, I fell in line with the guys walking but not in my normal position. Usually, I walked in close proximity to Sgt. Ferguson and a new second lieutenant by the name of Myers; but because I had to go back to get the morphine, nobody waited for me. The march continued forward. I was now more in the middle of the pack, not up front where I normally traveled. We hadn't gone far when a burst of withering gunfire knocked Leroy Ferguson down. A few other guys were wounded and lying near Ferguson. Bullets started flying all over. Compared to the normal firefight, this confrontation was different because of the huge amount of extremely loud firepower directed toward us.

Someone, probably Lt. Spencer, called for everyone to withdraw, and withdraw we did just as fast as we could! When we regrouped, word went out that Ferguson and others had been hit. Lieutenant Myers asked for three volunteers to go get Sgt. Ferguson. Because it was my job to attend to the wounded, I quickly volunteered. In the fog of war, I don't recall who else chose to go with me, but other guys definitely did volunteer. The term "fog of war" is an apt way to describe events in battle because they often merged together so that you couldn't tell one from another. We had to contend with so much coming at us from all directions—adrenaline, fear, temperatures over 100 degrees, the stress of battle, someone trying to kill you. This combination of forces alone kicks you into a different gear mentally and emotionally. I do know we low-crawled towards Ferguson and were observed by the enemy. We were fired at and sought cover low to the ground. I know I was as low as my body could possibly go. One guy was wounded, and I had to drag him back and administer first aid. We went out a second time, and the same thing happened. I dragged another wounded guy back. The effort to get to Ferguson at the moment was called off, but the battle raged on.

One of my buddies, Bob Harris, was positioned in a machine-gun hole firing at the enemy with an M-60 when I heard someone scream, "Medic!" Though I was administering aid to someone else at the time, perhaps a victim of heat exhaustion, I rushed to the area where I heard the voice. The voice I heard in the thick of the raging battle was Bob's. He'd been hit in the lower shoulder area and was in great pain. Someone in authority said to give him morphine, so I reached for a syringe. These syringes required that you put one tiny end into another. This was difficult to do because my hands were shaking. I had never given a morphine injection before, and I was terrified. Somehow, I was able to calm myself down and give Bob the needed injection. I kept telling him we'd get him out of there as soon as we could and that he would be okay. A medevac was on its way. Bob's response during the whole time he lay there was to say over and over, "I love my wife, I love my wife, I love my wife." Almost fifty years later, I remember this moment almost as vividly as when it happened. For years, in my ravaged mind, I thought Bob had died in my arms. But I later learned that Bob had been loaded on a chopper and passed away on the way to a treatment facility. When I think of this very sad day and Bob's words as he lay dying, I realize that no woman has been loved more than Bob Harris's wife; and she may have never known that.

After a while on Hill 352, I was racing everywhere with no regard for my safety. My survival instincts had failed me. I went everywhere I was called. The intense heat caused us to lose several guys to heat exhaustion. Were their heat exhaustion complaints all legitimate? Or, did some fake it? I don't know. I do know that some guys did do whatever they could to avoid being in the field. We had a name for these guys. They were called "shammers." Nobody in our company wanted to be where we were on that day, so it could well be that some of the guys I treated were shammers.

The battle on Hill 352 went on from morning until late afternoon. The fighting was very intense. Guys were dropping everywhere. The causes ran the gamut from getting hit by machine gun, mortars or rifle fire to suffering from heat exhaustion. In trying to attend to each of them, I had no time to take care of myself. I sent so many guys out on medevac that I lost count. Choppers were coming and going all day.

As I was taking care of all the guys, the new medic who'd arrived that day, was filling out the tags. The next thing I knew, someone was saying, "Get him out of there and put him on a chopper." It took a minute for me to realize that they were talking about me. In the extreme temperatures, I had become so dehydrated that I no longer knew what I was doing. I was almost delirious. I was told later that I'd been put on a helicopter but had jumped off the other side and watched it take off. Then I resumed trying to help the guys. Apparently, I told someone that I didn't want to leave my guys. Lieutenant Spencer saw me again administering aid and asked, "What's this guy still doing out here?" He instructed others to make sure I got out on the next chopper and that I stayed there. Though I continued to try to help, I was no longer competent. I was put on a chopper and as I found out later, I had been secured by Sergeant First Class Maene, who feared that in my delirium I would try and jump out of the chopper while airborne.

I vaguely remember the chopper landing and medical aid men dressed in white coming out to get me. Someone later told me that I slugged one of those guys and then passed out. When I awoke, I had needles in both arms, getting much needed fluids into my body. Because I had been fighting with the medical staff (unbeknownst to me), my arms were strapped to a medical cart. I couldn't move. When the fluids started taking hold, Lt. Spencer, who had likely suffered a wound of some kind, walked by me and, reportedly, complimented me on doing a remarkable job on the battlefield and said he would be recommending me for an award for bravery. At the time, feeling helpless, I was so exhausted and demoralized that his comment meant nothing to me.

I stayed at this medical facility for a few days. When I returned to my unit, I learned that, of the 100 guys we had sent up Hill 352, only twenty-nine came back down. For Charlie Company, the battle lasted for two days. Delta Company then picked up the battle and, with the help of others, were able to retake the hill.

When I got back with my unit, I was mentally, emotionally and physically drained. When I rejoined the guys in my platoon, I sensed that they were acting indifferent toward me. I thought at the time that their distance had something to do with my not staying out there with them. In my mind, I was telling myself that I had no control of the medevac decision. As it turns out, I was wrong about my perception of what the guys were feeling. We had just taken such a fierce ass-whipping that it had kicked the shit out of all them. Sure, we had been mortared, and we had been in numerous firefights and ambushes, but this had been our first major battle against the 2nd Division of the North Vietnamese Army. And we hoped it would be our last.

In May of 1968, after this horrible fight on Hill 352, I noticed that, of those who'd been with us since 1967 when the unit came over and 1968 when Al Torsiello and I arrived, very few were still with us. I did not recognize many of the guys out in the field anymore. After getting nearly decimated on Hill 352, we were getting replacement after replacement. They were strangers to me now; and because they were strangers, I didn't feel the same way about them as I did about the old timers. It didn't help that by this time I was emotionally numb. My experience on Hill 352 changed me forever.

Post Hill 352

F OLLOWING OUR ACTION AT HILL 352, we conducted search-
and-destroy operations around Tam Ky. We walked
through more than one village that we'd burned to the ground
only to be ambushed later down the road, likely in retribution for
what we'd done. We didn't just arbitrarily light these villages.
The order came down from above to burn the villages down
because these people had apparently ignored our relocation
efforts. We'd get our Zippo lighters out and start lighting the
roofs so the structures would burn. More than one *mamasan*
looked at us with hatred in her eyes. So much for winning the
hearts and minds of the people.

One afternoon, we stopped on a hill and noticed what appeared
to be launching areas for Viet Cong or NVA mortars. To us, it
looked like it could have been once used as a mortar launching
pad. As we looked over the area with greater interest, within
moments, we heard the distinctive sound of mortar canisters going
down enemy mortar tubes. Someone yelled "incoming" and, since
I was at the top of the hill, I wanted to clear out of the area
immediately and look for a spot where I could find protection.

Thinking the enemy had zeroed in on the top of the hill with
measurements for their mortar fire, and that they would start
dropping them very close to the landing pads, I began running
down the hill. While making my way down, I saw some guys

assembled in a man-made ditch. When a mortar exploded on top of the hill, I almost jumped on top of the guys. But the hole appeared to be full, so I hesitated for a second or two. I thought that if I'd just lie on top of them, I'd be lower than the shrapnel spray and then it would take a direct hit to get to me. However, something told me to go lower on the hill. Maybe I was just scared and thought I could out-run the mortar rounds. As it turns out, I did go lower on the hill, a decision that may have saved my life.

In a few moments, one of the enemy mortars landed almost right on top of the hole where I was going to seek refuge on top of the guys. I heard someone scream for a medic. I followed the direction of that sound and ran to the scene. The wounds I encountered were so severe and jagged from the sharp shrapnel, and the scene was so bloody that I involuntarily turned away from these wounded guys, took a few steps back and wretched. I was horrified at what I'd just seen. Then someone screamed at me directly saying, "Help them, man. It's your job!" Of course, I hadn't forgotten that helping the wounded was my job; but for a brief moment, I was unable to act. Embarrassed by my momentary lapse, I immediately gathered myself together and rendered aid to those severely wounded fellow soldiers who were then medevaced out.

After the mortar attack, I thought a lot about how close I'd come again to being severely maimed or killed. Even though I turned my back on the wounded for only a few seconds, I continued to beat myself up about it.

I don't know what the psychological term is for my momentary failure to help my comrades amid all the madness. Maybe it was severe shock that made me freeze. Whatever it was, I can only say that, for a moment, I did not have the stomach for what I had seen.

Ambush

OUR COMPANY CONTINUED THE search-and-destroy missions. One day, we were walking down a trail, and we saw a couple of enemy soldiers. Then we watched as they darted back into the brush. Al told me, after the fact, that he and his fellow infantrymen had been trained to look out for this exact scenario. As he described it, the enemy would show themselves, seemingly unintentionally, and then disappear. Our platoon ran after them and, almost immediately after, we were ambushed and pinned down with rapid gunfire. It was due only to the heroism of Sergeant First Class Artenio Romero, Jr., who had been able to sneak behind the ambushers and almost single handedly kill them all, that we were able to escape the ambush.

Because of Sgt. Romero and his steadying influence, we did not suffer major casualties that day. Though he was small in stature, he was able to save lives. He was so tough that we used to say that he had "balls of steel."

As a unit, though, it didn't seem that we were operating on all cylinders. After all, many of our veterans were gone, and we had new, inexperienced guys trying to fill in for them. Also, we weren't consistently following infantry strategies and employing guys out on the flanks. In a sense, we were a beaten unit, and we all knew it. This doesn't explain why we walked out of that first ambush into a second one not far down the road. None of us expected to get ambushed again, but that's exactly what happened. Fortunately, the enemy had sprung the ambush earlier than they should have, and we were able to fight our way out of it, again without major casualties. Had the enemy closed off all of the avenues of escape, we could have all been wiped out.

At this time, we were feeling vulnerable, to say the least. We walked ahead to a clearing just so we could catch our breath and regroup. Before we knew it, the enemy hit us for the third time, this time with a mortar ambush. They had the clearing area zeroed in on, and they let the mortars fly. As soon as I heard the canisters go down the tube, I moved out of the clearing and fought my way uphill through some thick brush and sought protection. I climbed until I could go no farther. All of us were like rabbits just running scared for what seemed like the hundredth time. Either Sgt. Romero or one of the lieutenants called in fire support in the direction of the mortar launchers, so we were able to extricate ourselves from our third ambush in one day. As horrible as these ambushes were, we lost very few guys that day, an outcome I'd attribute to the strong leadership of Sgt. Romero. No doubt others would agree. It was a day that I will never forget. After the war, people would tell me that they were having a bad day, and I would often respond by saying, "Try surviving three ambushes in one day."

Author (*center*) "taking five" with other soldiers, 1968.

Author (*far right*) securing a Vietcong prisoner.

Author getting cooled off by Mamasan.

On a MEDCAP mission in a Vietnamese village.

Author (right) playing "The Sandbag Blues" with Gary Jacobson.

Author with a Vietnamese child during a MEDCAP mission.

Jim Purtell in Chu Lai, 1969.

Captain Barney

I N THE THIRD WEEK OF MAY, WE HAD AN artillery captain leading us because so many of our infantry officers had been wounded in action or rotated. Lieutenant Spencer, who was with us for many battles including Hill 352, had rotated out of the field and was now the executive officer for Charlie Company at LZ Bayonet. Our captain, derisively called "Barney" (as in Barney Fife from the "Andy Griffith Show"), was a trained artillery officer; but he had no experience leading an infantry unit. Though he knew nothing at all about infantry operations, he was all we had. On many occasions, several of us vets disagreed with his strategies, but there was nothing we could do. He was in charge.

On or about May 21, 1968, we were walking down a dirt road, a main road in this particular area, and the captain passed the word to break for chow. We (mostly the older vets) were telling each other that we should not be walking on a main road without guys on the flank, nor should we be stopping for lunch on this road. We would definitely tip off the enemy what direction we were headed. Among ourselves, we talked about the fact that this wasn't the way we used to do things. We all thought that this was not going to end well.

After lunch, we resumed walking down the same road, still complaining about the captain's strategies. There was an area of ground at a higher elevation on our left that was potentially dangerous, and there was a low area on our right. At this time, we were working platoon-sized operations. Without our normal flank guys out there, our second platoon walked right into a small arms fire ambush. We fell to the ground and returned fire and, after a long time, fought our way out of the ambush. Several guys had suffered serious wounds and Jeff Segal had been killed, and I medevaced them all out. The captain had to have been hit too and was shipped out with these guys.

I then radioed LZ Bayonet to report the wounded in action and the killed in action. Whoever had been our radio person had been hit and shipped out that day, so I had to contact the company HQ and give them the WIA/KIA report. The person on the receiving end for Charlie Company knew how many guys we'd started out with for this operation. By the time I finished the report, he knew, but didn't say, that we had only fourteen guys left and not one was an officer. Those of us out in the bush knew we were in really rough shape. Late in the afternoon, we dug in relatively close to each other. We all knew we could die that night.

Nobody slept. We kept our eyes peeled for an enemy that fortunately never came. Al Torsiello and I were in the group of fourteen. He told me the next day that he spent the night in a hole with a Hispanic soldier who said the rosary all night long in low tones. We talked among ourselves about how shocked we were that the enemy hadn't attacked us that night. Had they done so, we would surely have been overrun and killed. Apparently, the enemy had no idea that there were only fourteen of us out there in the night.

Lieutenant Spencer, who had already completed his six-month rotation and didn't need or want to spend another minute in the field, gathered about four shammers, got them on a helicopter and came out to provide leadership. He led us out of the area, which was a very courageous thing for him to do. He didn't have to risk his life yet again, but he did. He did it for the fourteen of us who were still alive because he knew us all. With the help of the shammers and Lt. Spencer, we had five more rifles on that day to help with our exit.

Unfit for Duty

AS A RESULT OF BEING SHORT-STAFFED, and because of the continuous shit we had been engaged in and significant losses we'd suffered, someone much higher in rank, probably a general, determined that we were unfit—physically, mentally and emotionally—to continue operations in the field. A normal infantry company had about ninety men plus a fully staffed mortar platoon of another twenty-five guys, but we had difficulty fielding even sixty guys out in the bush. So our unit was lifted out of the field and taken to an extremely safe, light air missile battalion, a LAAM (land-to-air anti-missile site,) where we were treated to good food by Navy cooks and all the beer and liquor we could drink. We also had the opportunity to watch a few movies and get some rest. I suspect the idea behind this stand-down was to lift our spirits. Also, it would give the military leadership time to find replacements to field a full company. As I recall, we spent about a week to ten days there.

Avoid the Enemy

F OLLOWING OUR STAY AT THE LAAM SITES, our mission changed. We were no longer going to search for the enemy. In fact, because of our few members, we were told to avoid the enemy except for conducting night ambushes. During the day, we set up our perimeter. At night, we went out on patrols, or rat patrols as they were commonly called. We did have some successes with these night ambushes.

On one of the night ambushes, I had served my guard duty and handed it off to someone else. I asked the guy if he was awake and he said he was. So I went to sleep, but soon woke up. This guy, who was supposed to be standing guard, was snoring! I was so pissed off that I kicked him. I did not go back to sleep that night. My nerves were frayed. I had been going on these ambushes voluntarily. I wasn't required or expected to do so, which made me doubly angry at the guy who was supposed to be standing guard while I slept.

Within that same week, we opened fire on the enemy in an ambush situation; and one of our guys got hit. I heard a muffled call for a medic, but I froze. Up to this point, I had made it through almost five months of harrowing combat and survived a guy falling asleep on guard duty. All I had to do was to make it another month and I'd be rotated out of the field. Lying there, unable to move, I thought to myself that I didn't want to die. But, for some strange reason, I had the feeling that I was going to die if I moved. I can't explain why I felt this way on that particular night, but I did. Since I'd hesitated too long, a young infantryman stepped up, went and got the guy and carried him back. I was ashamed of myself for not acting, and I have carried this shame with me ever since.

According to others, I had many brave moments during my year of going through countless battles and firefights. But on this occasion, I failed myself and my fellow soldier. Almost five decades after the war, I still wish I could take that moment of failure back. Sadly, life doesn't afford us do-overs.

Mortar Platoon

I N EARLY JUNE OF 1968, I HAD SERVED with the second platoon for so long that I really didn't know anyone who'd been in country for any length of time except for my buddy Al. I was asked to serve with the mortar platoon for awhile, so I accepted that assignment because they still had some of the old timers left. The reason for this is because they were almost always situated on a safer hill, and they weren't plodding through a jungle full of booby traps, nor were they subject to ambushes or as many firefights, at least as the infantry guys were exposed to. But, to my surprise, when I joined the mortar platoon, our commander at the time thought the mortar platoon should travel with the infantry platoons, so I hadn't really improved my hand.

We tried this experiment for awhile, but it was very clumsy carrying mortar tubes, the mortar base and mortar rounds. It was very loud as we traveled through the boonies. Unlike the infantry guys, the mortar guys just didn't have the expertise or the experience walking through the bush. It was just plain loud out there, and I and several others felt that we were signaling with our noise exactly where we were headed. Eventually, it was decided that the mortar platoon should return to a forward base where we could be more effective. Since I was assigned to them, I went to the forward base where it was much safer.

My time with the mortar platoon gave me an opportunity to write letters home. I wrote to Donna and to my parents and some friends. Since I'd been getting fewer and fewer letters from Donna, I knew something bad was up. I figured she wanted to break up with me but didn't know how to do it. I would often joke with the guys about "Dear John" letters, but I never expected to get one. Receiving letters from home was the lifeblood for soldiers. When the helicopters came in to resupply us, they would throw a mailbag down, and the staff sergeant would grab a bunch of envelopes and call out the names of those who had mail. Not receiving a letter from home was depressing. You felt as if no one cared about you.

Sometimes, guys would receive boxes from home, or care packages, as we called them. They would share what they got with their closer buddies. Common within these care packages sent from home was Kool Aid. Of course, that powdered drink required water. When we weren't regularly supplied, we often got our water out of the rice paddies or rivers. We had to take precautions, though, so that leeches didn't make their way into our canteens. We would flush any debris out of the way in the water source and insert the canteen into the water spreading two fingers over the opening, creating a slit large enough for water to get in, but nothing else. When the canteen was almost full, we'd pull it out of the water and then pour in a package of Kool Aid and a disinfectant pill. We'd shake it up and have warm Kool Aid to drink. It beat the taste of rice-paddy or river water, which is why it was one of the most requested commodities.

While I was with the mortar platoon on some hill, Al was with the second platoon. On June 3, 1968, his unit was hit by a devastating mortar attack. He told me he heard the rounds as they were coming through the air. He was looking for a safe spot when he came upon a wily veteran, Dave Provost, smiling under a tree.

Al said that he almost jumped in with Provost, but for reasons he couldn't explain, he continued running. It was probably the sheer terror that overcomes you when you know your life is on the line. A mortar hit the tree that Provost was under, and it shot straight down through his helmet killing him instantly. Provost was one of the smartest, most savvy enlisted guys we knew. His loss haunted all of us who knew him. Some of us thought he was one of the best soldiers we'd ever met (next to career Sgt. Romero). We wondered what our chances of staying alive in this godforsaken country were, given that another one of our top infantry guys had been killed. Sergeant Tom Blades, Specialist Andy Thomas and 2nd Lieutenant Michael Wilson were all killed in this mortar attack. All of these losses occurred in a matter of minutes; another sad day for our company.

Back to the Bush

I STAYED WITH THE MORTAR COMPANY through June of 1968. In July, I was moved back to one of the infantry platoons. I don't remember if I was assigned to the first or third platoon. Maybe I moved back and forth between the two. For some strange reason July 1968 was not an active month for fatalities. I know we were involved in fire fights, but fortunately no one in our company lost his life in July. While in Vietnam, I never kept a log because, at the time, I did not want to remember what had happened there. So this entire account is coming completely from my memory. I do know that in August, I should have been rotated back to LZ Bayonet, but that didn't happen. The excuse I heard was that they had no one to replace me. In August and going into September, we went back out on our search missions. Our numbers were still low. Also, we'd lost a few new officers in several firefights. For a few weeks, we were leaderless. We had no officer in the field.

When Colonel Kelly became aware of the situation, he offered a young sergeant a field commission to second lieutenant. Sergeant Jim Stringham refused the commission because he didn't want to be an officer. However, Sgt. Stringham said he'd do the best he could to lead us on our operations. And like Sgt. Romero, Jim Stringham had balls of steel. They were both great soldiers and leaders.

With the exception of Spencer and Carrier, Sergeants Romero
and Stringham were better than most officers we had during my
year in Vietnam. As I recall, Sgt. Romero led the first platoon
and Sgt. Stringham led the third platoon. Or, it could be that both
of them managed all three platoons. It doesn't matter how the
leadership was set up. The main thing is that these two sergeants
were exceptional.

Obviously, losing leaders adversely affected morale. In the
military, we had all been trained to follow leaders. In an infantry
company in the field, you had a captain and at least three
lieutenants for the first, second and third platoons. Then there
was a staff sergeant for each platoon. Yet, we no longer had a
captain, or any lieutenants or staff sergeants. Instead we were
being lead by one career sergeant and one non-career sergeant,
enlisted men who had been promoted through the ranks.

LZ Center

FOR SOME REASON, DURING THIS PERIOD, we were in LZ Center running missions from this fortified position down the hill into outlying areas. At night, from inside the perimeter, we sent parachute flares up into the sky so they would light up the area to include our bunkers and the concertina razor wire around our perimeter. This, I believe, was called harassment and interdictment (H&I). These flares were shot up by our howitzers or mortars, the purpose being to ward off night time attacks by the enemy. Usually, we found these very comforting because whoever was on guard could scan the area with the best light we could manufacture. Then, if the enemy was observed, we could fire on them.

On one night, the enemy must have felt they knew our cycle for timing these illumination flares, so they tried to penetrate our barbed wire enclosure. Our cycle for sending these flares was every half hour or forty-five minutes. The enemy may have felt that they could begin their advance after the last flare fizzled out. But some wise armor officer decided to alter the cycle that night. Instead of every forty-five minutes, he decided to send a flare up out of schedule at, say, the fifteen minute mark. As a result, our people on guard sighted enemy soldiers who had almost made their way through the barbed wire and, within minutes, would have been upon us inside our camp. We opened fire and caught some of the enemy entangled in the wire. They died at the point in the wire where they had advanced.

The next morning, we went to the barbed wire perimeter and saw seven or eight dead North Vietnamese Army soldiers. If one of those soldiers had made it through the wire undetected, he could have created some real havoc. If seven or eight had made it through in a coordinated effort, there would have been massive casualties and some would likely have been by friendly fire. In the pitch-black night, locating seven or eight guys within our encampment would have been very difficult. Sure, you could detect where shots were coming from, but would it be safe to shoot at them, not knowing what was behind them? Fortunately for us, they got caught in the wire.

I have a vague memory of guys having gone through the dead soldiers' pockets looking for souvenirs, money or intelligence data. Then, due to the fear of disease, there was the question of what to do with all the dead bodies. An order went out to bury them, but that proved to be problematic because getting the bodies out of the barbed wire would desecrate them even more. Finally, we were told to pour diesel fuel over the bodies and burn them. The awful stench was a smell we wouldn't soon forget.

During this same period of time, we were conducting platoon-sized operations. We had made our way to the top of yet another hill and we formed a perimeter to establish our night position.

I'm sure the hill had a name, but on that night, to us, it was just another hill. It was dark. We were all dug in, and the most unusual thing happened. The enemy did not attack us with small arms fire. Rather, they attacked us by throwing hand grenades from positions just below us. Their grenades, which we called Chi-Coms, were of questionable reliability; but, still, many of them went off. Whoever was in charge that night radioed in for a gunship (an armed helicopter with tremendous firing power), because he was afraid we were going to be overrun. The enemy was already close enough to lob hand grenades at us, and there were so few of us. One landed very close to me and, fortunately, did not go off.

As the helicopter pilot approached our position, he saw a large enemy force ascending our hill. He asked those of us who had flashlights to point them to the sky towards him and, only then, turn them on so he could see exactly where we were situated. We did as we were told and then sat back to watch the best fireworks of our young lives. I don't know what the ratio was, but it seemed that every third or fourth round fired was an illuminated round. The gunners on the helicopters peppered the area outside of our flashlights, killing many of the enemy and forcing others to retreat. Our lives were saved yet again. These pilots and gunners were heroes to us and to those who were injured and needed to be medevaced. These guys were absolutely outstanding, and we had the highest respect for them. How could we not?

We were very lucky again that night because we had been vastly outnumbered by an overwhelming force. But for our radio communication technology and the weaponry on the helicopter gunship, we likely would have been overrun.

Take Another Hill

NOTHING PISSED OFF US OLD TIMERS more than receiving an order to take another hill. During my tour, we had taken some hills, then vacated them and, months later, had to take them again. What upset us most was the fact that we never secured these hills for any length of time. It looked to us like there was no coherent strategy in Vietnam. We'd take one hill and hump a long distance to a completely different area. Or, we were moved by large helicopters to the new area. It made no sense. It's no wonder we felt as expendable as we did. Our lives did not seem to matter one bit.

At the time, we were not aware that we were indeed pawns on a chessboard in a game played by some generals in Chu Lai or Da Nang.

On this hill that we were about to take, Staff Sgt. Romero called me, Sgt. Gomez-Mesa and a third guy, whose name I don't remember, to a short meeting. This was on the afternoon of August 31, 1968. Sergeant Romero explained to us that we had intelligence that said there was enemy on top of the hill. He let us know that we were definitely going to encounter resistance. I suspect that the reason I was called in to this meeting was because, by now, I was one of the most seasoned guys still out in the field. Still, it was unusual, I thought, for a medic to be involved in an infantry strategy meeting. Sergeant Romero told

Gomez-Mesa that he was going to walk point the next day. Gomez-Mesa protested because he'd just walked point the day before. He thought it was someone else's turn. Technically, he was right. Normally, we rotated guys at point. It was a very vulnerable position. Sergeant Romero told him that he was walking point because he knew where the enemy was. Gomez-Mesa protested further, saying that he had only thirteen days left in the Army and, therefore, shouldn't even be out there. He was right on that point too. In our unit, when infantry guys had two weeks left in Vietnam, they were usually pulled in from the field. I don't know why Gomez-Mesa hadn't been called in. It could have been a paperwork error. Or, maybe someone in the rear area thought we didn't have enough guys, and there would be fewer of us if he'd been called in.

It's important to remember that 1968 was the worst year of the war for the U.S. in terms of suffering casualties. There were 500,000 American troops in Vietnam. There were also troops from the Republic of Korea and Australia assisting the Americans. But a little known fact is that the majority of Americans involved in the war effort did not fight. The ratio of non-combatant to combatant was anywhere from eight to one to ten to one. This means that, of the 500,000 Americans in-country, only 80,000 of us were fighting in that year. The rest of the guys worked in jobs in intelligence, radio communication, supplies, kitchen, auto and jet mechanics. Some were airplane and helicopter personnel, hospital workers, financial and administrative people, etc. To us, they had cushy jobs in safe areas. Fairly or unfairly, we resented them immensely. As unrealistic as it was, our logic at the time was that these guys could have picked up a rifle and come out and helped us.

That resentment was part of the many intangibles that we carried with as we prepared to take yet another hill. On September

1, 1968, the morning after our meeting with Sgt. Romero, Sgt. Gomez-Mesa and Sgt. Busse approached me at different times. They asked if I would walk between them as we went up the hill. I said I would as long as Sgt. Romero agreed. From a tactical perspective, it was poor placement for me. When we were doing platoon-sized operations without an officer, I walked in the middle of the guys so I could move forward or in reverse, depending on where we got hit. Sergeant Romero did agree to this placement, a decision he may have made because the people involved were all old timers. Or, he may have agreed because of his concern for Gomez-Mesa, remembering his earlier decision to have him walk point.

I didn't know Gomez-Mesa or Dan Busse that well as they were with the third platoon. I really hadn't been with them long, maybe a day or two at most. Though I had seen them before when we had company-sized operations, we were now doing platoon-sized operations, which meant I'd been spending most of my time with the first or second platoon. Nevertheless, when Gomez-Mesa repeated to me that he had only thirteen days left in the Army and that if he got hit he'd want me close by, I said, "Okay."

Busse, who had just returned from R&R, said he had a bad feeling about this hill. He told me that he had only forty-five days left in Vietnam. He, too, asked if I'd walk close to him. Of course, I said yes. I agreed to it because I had a lot of respect for infantry guys who'd managed to survive after that much time in the bush. These truly seasoned guys were rare.

When we got the order to move out, we began making our way up the hill. As I recall, Gomez-Mesa was first, I was second and Busse third. I'm not sure but I may have walked behind Busse in the third position. In any event, I was very close to them, just as they'd asked me to be. There has been some dispute about who actually went up the hill first. Others on this operation have said that a soldier by the name of Hooper went up first. That may well have been. It could also be the case that Gomez-Mesa asked someone else to walk point after our meeting with Sgt. Romero. I'm only telling this story as I recall it. In the whole scheme of things, who walked point on that afternoon doesn't matter. All I know for sure is that I was very close to Busse and Gomez-Mesa.

Certain parts of Vietnam were mountainous. What we were taking could have been a small mountain range, but we called them all hills. As we slowly moved up, we got no resistance from the enemy. When we got to the top, Gomez moved to the left and Busse followed him, keeping a proper distance of about ten feet between them. Instead of following them off to the left, I kept walking straight and ended up about eight to ten feet to the right of Busse.

Glancing quickly, I saw that the top of the hill had once contained a dense area of trees which had all been removed. From my vantage point, I could see a sea of tree stumps bordered by thick vegetation. There may have been an opening among these stumps where the ground was flat. It would make sense because these trees had been removed to create an LZ. The tree stumps made it difficult to move because we had to concentrate, to a certain extent, on our feet to navigate them.

Throughout my time in the field, we were always warned to spread out and keep a proper distance between yourself and the person behind and in front of you. This way, if we were ambushed, the enemy would get some but not all of us. The same reasoning applied to a mortar attack. A round could take out four or five guys, but one round was not going to take out twenty guys.

As we walked on top of this particular hill, with the proper distance between us, an enemy machine gunner, who seemed to be positioned to our right and hidden by the vegetation, opened up and shot at us from his right to his left. Sergeant Gomez-Mesa was hit in the head and killed instantly. At the first sign of gunfire, I immediately dropped in place and sought refuge behind the largest tree stump I could find. Bullets were flying all around and hitting the dirt near me. I put my fingers together, intertwined them in front of my steel pot helmet hoping that, if I were to be shot in the head area, the bullet would hit the bones in my hand and be diverted in a different direction but not go through my head. I then heard a cry of help and looked to my left and saw that Busse had been hit in the heart, and blood was gushing out of his chest with tremendous force.

To this day, I have never forgotten the look on his face. He was staring right at me with a desperate, pleading look. I'm sure I was the last guy he ever saw.

I was locked in or pinned down within the stumps. Given the machine gun fire, I felt that if I'd poked my head up above the stump, I would be a dead man. Despite the fact that Busse was only eight or ten feet away, there were several three-foot-high tree stumps between us. Thinking about this experience after many years, I still feel that I would have been killed had I lifted my head above the stump. This machine gunner (and who knows how many other enemy had set up in the area) had already killed one guy, Sgt. Gomez-Mesa; and Dan Busse was dying. Though I was sure that Busse had suffered a mortal wound, I still wanted to get to him so I could try to do something for him. So I started inching backward thinking I could get back far enough without opening myself to the shooter. I'd hoped that I could find another lane within the stumps to get to Busse. I soon discovered that this too was impossible because of the stumps behind me. I pulled out a knife and began cutting into a small stump near me, thinking (foolishly as it turned out) that I could create a lane to get to Busse. Before long, the firing stopped. Then the troops from behind came forward. The fight was over. We lost Gomez-Mesa,

Dan Busse, Steve O'Hara and Roger Shrewsbury—all killed in action within minutes.

I turned over on my back and, for the very first time, cried for all of the guys I had seen get wounded and for Captain Hurtado and Bob Harris and Leroy Ferguson and Jeff Segal and Gomez-Mesa, especially for Dan Busse and Steve O'Hara and Roger Shrewsbury. I lay there on my back until a lieutenant, probably Lt. Meyers, yelled that we were moving out. Reluctantly, I got up and began walking as the tears just kept coming.

When we assessed things later, one of our guys said he saw someone in a green uniform running from the area. It's possible that one enemy soldier, armed with a machine gun, had done all the damage.

Monsoons/Leeches/
Elephant Grass/Prickers/
Mosquitoes

A S ALL OF THIS BRUTAL ACTION WAS taking place, we were also having to contend with day-to-day hardships. Our daily lives were definitely a lot harder to endure than the lives of the non-combatants, a fact that contributed to the resentment we had for the guys in rear area.

One of these hardships had to do with monsoons. In our part of Vietnam, the monsoon season ran from May/June to October. The Central Highlands where we operated seemed to have the larger and longer downpours. It rained and rained and rained. It would stop for periods and then rain some more. Sometimes, you couldn't see more than a few feet in front of you. Typically, we'd like to find an area under cover and hunker down and send out patrols from that newly discovered base. When it rained hard, it seemed to us as if the enemy had hunkered down just as we did, and there were periods of inaction, which we didn't mind one bit.

I recall one evening in the mountains sitting on a large rock and leaning against another rock. To keep dry, I was wearing my poncho. Because I was utterly exhausted, I slept upright in that position for the night. Out in the field, it was next to impossible to get enough sleep when we lay down at night.

The monsoon season was hard on the soldiers who'd set up in the jungle areas. Without the monsoons, the jungles smelled as if they were in a continuous rotting state. The dampness was constant. Add the rains and another problem arose. We had to keep checking ourselves for leeches. When we lay down to sleep before our shift of guard duty, we could be on top of a poncho on the jungle floor, yet somehow these leeches made their way to the moist, hairy parts of our bodies while we slept. We would awaken and find them on our heads, under armpits and in the groin or genitals area. To remove them in the mornings, we would light a cigarette and place it on them until they curled up and fell off. Also, mosquito repellant would do the trick. Guys would then grab them and throw them against the rocks; and, since they were blood suckers, they would splat with our blood.

One day, a new medic came out into the field in a clean uniform and black boots. He'd been told to see me. I was sitting down with buddies eating some C-Rats. We'd just been through another horrible round of shit, and I was dead tired. It was raining. When the new guy approached me, he said, "Do you know you have leeches all over your arms?" Without lifting my head to look at him or greet him, I said, "They'll fall off when they've sucked enough blood." This was my sarcastic way of welcoming newbies to the field. At this point, I was beyond feeling for these new guys. I can't imagine what he was thinking. This was probably his first "oh shit" moment.

Out in the field, we'd all had them.

****

It was close to impossible to stay dry during the monsoon season. Also, despite our being in a relatively hot environment, the nights, especially in the mountains, could get cool. So, there would be nights when we would end up wet and shivering—one more layer of misery to add to the downpours and the leeches.

Almost everyone smoked cigarettes, myself included. We did so, in large part, because the government freely gave them to us out in the field. I guess they weren't going to deny us a tiny pleasure, so they kept us supplied just as they kept us supplied with food and water. When supplies came in on the chopper, we got C-rations, an occasional change of fatigues, mail and cigarettes. Cigarettes were a staple, but it was a challenge to keep them dry during the monsoons.

Added to our discomfort were the high grasses (which we called "elephant grass") found in the Central Highlands. Since we often walked through these areas during the day when it was very hot, we had our sleeves rolled up. Our exposed bare arms would invariably come in contact with the elephant grass, and it would cut our arms. They were such a constant nuisance. It was like getting a bunch of paper cuts. If guys didn't put on a medical ointment (and many shrugged it off), these cuts would fester and get infected. Elephant grass was just one more of the many annoying discomforts we had to deal with on a daily basis.

It seemed that every plant we encountered in Vietnam was like a rose bush with big prickers on them. We often moved through areas rather quickly. When we reached out to clear something out of the way, we would often find prickers sticking us in our arms or hands. These small cuts would get infected as well. Being in the jungle was just one more piss-off. There was nothing about being there that made it easy for guys to stay healthy.

In the jungle, we had to douse ourselves with mosquito repellant every night. We'd apply it to our faces, neck and hands, all exposed areas of our bodies. The Vietnam mosquitoes were huge! They weren't as big as tiny birds, although at times it seemed so; but they were a lot larger than we were used to back home. We'd go to sleep at night hearing their buzzing sound in our ears. They were looking for any open area to strike. These over-sized mosquitoes were a nightly hazard for us.

Many guys carried the mosquito repellant in their helmet liners; but I thought the white containers would make a great target for the enemy snipers, so I kept mine in my rucksack. Though the repellant worked great against mosquitoes and leeches, I thought that the smell of it gave away our position much like the enemy's rancid-smelling tobacco did for theirs.

R&R, Hookers and Pot

I N ANY WAR ZONE, THERE AREN'T MANY PLEASURES. AS I mentioned earlier, cigarettes were one pleasure, though a tiny one. It's important to remember that we were young and virile tough guys consumed with thoughts of women. At government-recognized rest and recreation sites, there were women from foreign countries. Each time a guy returned from a week of R&R in an exotic place like Japan, Thailand or Singapore (the married guys met their wives in Hawaii), we would get educated about the beautiful girls in that country. Newly returned guys could not talk enough about how beautiful the women were, how many were available and how you could choose the one you wanted. Often, guys would return with pictures of exotic girls the likes of which we'd never seen before. Most of us were used to round-eyed white girls or round-eyed black girls.

Now, these guys were showing us some very attractive Asian girls, and we were envious. Some guys bought Polaroid cameras at their R&R site and took semi-nude pictures which drove us all nuts when we saw them. Everyone who returned from R&R had stories to tell. Even if they hadn't really experienced the girls, they had heard enough stories to lie and present something believable. Needless to say, we all looked forward to R&R.

I went to Sydney, Australia; yet, my experience was less than ideal. Because I didn't pay close attention to the "non-potable" water sign in Da Nang and drank the water, I used an air sickness bag all the way to Sydney.

But what about girlfriends in the States? The Army actually did us a favor by introducing us to "Jody-themed" songs in basic training. "Jody" was the bastard who stole girlfriends and wives from soldiers while we were away. Back in Basic Training, when we'd be marching, the DIs would have cadenced stories about Jody that all ended the same way: "Jody got your girl." The reason that this was a favor to us was because many guys lost their girlfriends and wives while serving in Vietnam. At least we were minimally prepared for it to happen to us. There were plenty of Jody's ready and willing to steal our wives or girlfriends.

One of the things we did was to learn the names of the wives and girlfriends of our fellow soldiers and say that, when we got back to the States, we were going to look them up and take care of them (sexually) for the other guy until he got home. We constantly ribbed each other, but some guys were very sensitive about it. Most often, these were the guys who got the most ribbing. It was all good-natured, though. At least at our emotional and psychological levels, we thought it was. This kind of bantering was mixed in with the normal everyday pissing and moaning that helped us to endure life in a war zone.

****

In some of the popular villages in Vietnam, Anton being one, there were girls of ill-repute who would provide services to almost all soldiers for five dollars. As Paul Simon says in his song "The Boxer": *I do declare there were times I was so lonesome I took some comfort there.*" Most of us were eighteen or nineteen years old and making $300 a month while we were in Vietnam. This included $90 of combat pay. To put this amount into perspective, we were risking our lives for an additional three dollars a day over our regular pay. With the infantry, we had nowhere to go to spend our money, and we sorely missed contact with women. We knew we could be dead at anytime, so it was easy to rationalize spending our money this way. As in every war, there were women who were trying to improve themselves financially and women who were opportunists and were available to meet the needs of soldiers. Though I don't know this for sure, I presume these girls were scorned by their community. It could be that the opposite was the case since these women were bringing an income to their extremely poor families. In this environment, the rules of everyday life no longer applied because there might not be a tomorrow for us. When you think of it in these terms, it is much easier to understand.

Another form of pleasure was marijuana, which I was introduced to by a guy we called Gypsy, a Puerto Rican I'd patched up five different times and who was awarded, I believe, five Purple Hearts, each one well deserved. When he got back to New York, he wrote me a letter thanking me for patching him up, the term we used when a medic cleaned and bandaged a wound caused by enemy fire. Gypsy was a very brave guy, a tunnel rat who seemed fearless. He was one of the original guys who came over with Louie Pantaleone, Ed McCracken, Scott, Provost, Gene "Bean" Lynch and others in the second platoon whose names I don't recall.

I remember well, though, how it was that Gypsy got me to try marijuana. We were on a short stand-down at LZ Bayonet where we had no responsibilities. I was walking around looking for some of our guys. I poked my head into one bunker, and Gypsy said quietly, "Doc, come on in." When I went in, I saw that there were some others there, all with big smiles on their faces. I couldn't figure out what was going on, so I asked. Gypsy said, "Doc, now you have to be cool." I assured him that I was. Then he said, "Take a hit on this." Since I trusted Gypsy, I took a hit on the marijuana stick, a joint sold in villages for one dollar a stick, larger than an American cigarette but smaller than a cigar. I took a hit and started coughing like crazy. Everyone laughed at my inexperience.

"Doc, you have to do it like this," Gypsy said. He inhaled on a joint and told me to hold the smoke in my lungs and then let it out slowly. He cautioned me not to take too much. So I tried it again, and soon I was smiling like the rest of them. We were all laughing when a sergeant came in, no doubt because he noticed the pungent smell and heard us cracking up. He had a stern look on his face as he looked around to see who was there. Once he recognized us as combat vets, he told us not to be smoking that stuff, and then he left.

While I was in the infantry, I didn't know of anyone who smoked marijuana out in the field, but we thought in this one instance inside the base camp had been harmless. Since I had to be alert at all times, I certainly never smoked out there. I demanded that alertness of myself, and my infantry comrades felt the same way. Besides, there was no way that we could hide that distinct smell from each other or the enemy.

I've Got to Get out of This Place

AFTER OUR SEVERE LOSSES ON SEPTEMBER 1, 1968, I called LZ Bayonet on the radio and told them that I'd spent more than six months out in the field and that I wanted to be rotated out as I'd been promised by Sgt. Webb. I pleaded with someone in Headquarters Company, explaining that I'd had more than my share of shit, and I wanted to be treated fairly. Like all medics, I was a *member* of Headquarters but only *assigned* to Charlie Company. The person I spoke with said he'd do his best to get me out.

The Army actually did us a disservice in telling us medics in our company that after six months in the field, we would be rotated to the rear area. I believed what I'd heard from Sgt. Webb. Having spent well over six months in the field, I wanted them to honor their word and rotate me out. If they'd said I had to spend eight months out in the field, I would have served eight months and wanted out once that eight months was up. But they told me six months was the length of time I'd be out there. Having reminded them that I'd gone past my six months, I was told that they would look for a replacement for me.

Several weeks later, doing the same old war shit, I got word that I was going to get rotated out and that my replacement was coming on the next chopper. I saw the smoke that signaled for the helicopter to land, quickly said goodbye to the guys and ran to the helicopter just as this other soldier got off. I assumed he was my replacement, a new medic, but he wasn't. He said, "The guy they had lined up to replace you just re-upped and was shipped to Germany. "You're fucking shitting me," I shouted. No, he was not. I walked back to the guys I'd just said goodbye to and told them the story. "Man, this fucking Army," they said. Naturally, I was very depressed about the situation, depressed and pissed off as well. But I knew there was nothing I could do. Once again, I accepted an involuntary extension of my assignment— reluctantly.

September of 1968 turned into October, and I was working my eighth month in the field. I had served a longer time than any other medic I knew. Having heard that medics have the shortest lifespan of anyone in Vietnam, I was chomping at the bit to get out. Then I was notified that a replacement had been found, and this time it was for real.

Waiting for the chopper to come in, I half expected to get shafted again, but this time it didn't happen. I shook the new medic's hand—I may have even hugged him—and got on the helicopter as fast as I could. On the way back to LZ Bayonet, I thought about all of my combat experiences, the guys I was leaving behind and all of the buddies who had been injured or killed in action.

How relieved and grateful I was to be getting out with all of my limbs and my brain intact. A short time later, I landed at LZ Bayonet.

LZ Bayonet Revisited

A T LZ BAYONET, I REPORTED TO Headquarters Company and was processed in again. I was told I would be assigned to the Medical Clinic where I would begin working the following day. My living quarters were a few rows away from the Clinic. This is where I'd be spending the next four months.

LZ Bayonet was a large sea of tents, and I was assigned to an area in the medics' hooch, which was right next door to the officers' hooch. Each tent was about twenty feet wide and thirty to forty feet long with sandbags stacked three feet high surrounding each one. Basically, all of the medics who were finished with their six months of field requirements were situated in the same tent, so we got to know each other very well. Having all gone through similar experiences, we understood and respected one another. We were given an Army-issued cot, some screen netting to ward off mosquitoes and a foot locker for our personal belongings. That was it.

Bathrooms, as I recall, were glorified outhouses. Showers were small tent enclosures with a fifty-gallon barrel of water above, which was occasionally warm. We were instructed to get wet when showering, turn off the water and soap up. Then we were to rinse off the soap. It was important to conserve water for the rest of the guys.

Because I left from LZ Bayonet to go to the field from there, I was pretty familiar with my surroundings. Also, sometimes we were brought in there for a few days between operations. LZ Bayonet had an enlisted men's club, an officers' club and a mess hall where everyone took their meals. I spent many an evening at the enlisted men's club trying to drown my sorrows, and I had plenty of company.

At the Medical Clinic, I worked for Doctor Patterson. Not only was he a good physician, but he was also a pretty damn good quarterback. After work—we held normal hours—we had touch football games at LZ Bayonet. Because Dr. Patterson was an officer, he was able to use his rank to get the quarterback position he wanted. He and I developed a very good rapport on the football field. I had been a wide receiver/halfback in high school, and I was blessed with good hands. I also knew how to run solid pass patterns and give a defender a head or shoulder fake. Often, Dr. Patterson would look for me, and I would be open for long touchdown passes. It was strange to think that we were playing football at a base camp while, a few miles away, guys were getting killed in the field. It was hard to wrap my head around this. Where we were was safe, and the war was somewhere out there. At the time, I never considered that I had become what we hated when we were out in the field—a guy with a cushy job in a safe place.

The medics' hooch had the only refrigerator at LZ Bayonet, other than the ones in the mess hall. Though some medications required refrigeration, not many did. This left plenty of room for cold beer. Since the officers' hooch was right next to ours, everyday after work we had a happy hour, a time when officers would let down their guard and rank, and mix with us enlisted guys. In the States, there was no fraternization allowed between officers and enlisted men; but in Vietnam, at least where we were, we mixed easily. The officers knew we controlled the injection cards of every soldier. All a medic would have to say was that it would be easy to lose an injection card. Losing one of these cards meant that a soldier would need to get several injections before leaving the country. The fact that the officers knew this might have also contributed to the special relationship between medics and officers.

Lieutenant Calley

I N NOVEMBER OR DECEMBER OF 1968, a new officer, William Rusty Calley, joined the hooch next door. We called him "Rusty." He had been assigned to Echo Company of the 1/6th 198th Infantry Brigade, which was a unique and small group of guys who performed recon functions. They would go out on operations, locate the enemy and report back so other larger infantry companies, like Charlie Company, could attack those positions. We didn't really know anyone from Echo Company, and why Calley was next door was a mystery to me. But I never gave it much thought. Since he had a cot in the officers' hooch, I just assumed he was with Headquarters Company like everyone else.

At happy hour, we often had beers together; and having been assigned a medical jeep, I drove Lt. Calley to Anton village one day to find a young woman to clean his quarters. He selected one, and I drove them back to LZ Bayonet. After a few hours, he asked me to return her to the village, and I did. It appeared to me by the look on her face that she hadn't been cleaning his quarters. Calley later told me with a grin that he hadn't had her there to clean.

Despite the fraternization between officers and enlisted men, the officers still knew how to give orders. I interacted with Lt. Calley daily for a couple of months, at least in our happy hour sessions, where he was considered just one of the guys. During these happy hours, Lt. Calley and I would talk. In December 1968, when he was headed back home, which I believe was Georgia, he told me he intended to make the Army his career because he liked it. When he left, I wished him good luck, like I did every soldier I knew and liked. I thought I'd never see or hear from him again.

It was not until I was back in the States that I, and the rest of the world, heard about him again. In 1969 the news of the My Lai Massacre broke. Because of his actions at My Lai, he became the most infamous soldier of the entire Vietnam War. Lieutenant William "Rusty" Calley was charged with twenty-two counts of murder, and he became the key figure in the investigation. In 1971, President Nixon ordered him transferred from Leavenworth prison to house arrest at Fort Benning, pending appeal. He served three and a half years of the house arrest and was eventually released a free man (although with a general court martial and dishonorable discharge on his record) in 1974.

Bac Si

A BOUT EVERY TWO WEEKS OR SO, I would go into local villages by jeep, often by myself, because some areas were considered very safe. The purpose of these trips was to administer medical aid to the local people. The Army was operating under a policy to win the hearts and minds of the Vietnamese people, and these medical visits were part of that program. Each medic assigned to the Medical Clinic performed this service.

When I arrived in villages, I would tell one of the villagers that I was a medic. They used the term *Bac Si*, which meant "doctor." Obviously, I was not a doctor; but for many of these villagers, I was the closest thing to it. Once my presence was announced, there would be a line of people seeking treatment for themselves or their children. I would perform any medical service that I was trained for. I would clean sores and wounds with antiseptics and then apply a Neosporin-like ointment and bandage the persons. For those with more serious infections, I gave penicillin injections. If I were confronted with serious medical conditions beyond my qualifications and experience, I would get on the radio and call the Medical Clinic at LZ Bayonet and describe the patient's discussion.

Then the medical professional at LZ Bayonet and I would make a decision as to what could be done, if anything. Because I helped a lot of people to the extent that I could, I very much enjoyed these visits to the villages. For me, these visits restored some humanity that had been stripped out of me out in the jungles.

Short-Timer

MY HUMANITY WAS RESTORED EVEN further when, on February 12, 1969, I was informed that I would be leaving Vietnam the next day and that I had received a four-day drop. This meant that, instead of leaving on February 12 to correspond with my arrival on that same day a year ago, the Army was allowing me to depart four days earlier. I started telling guys I was really "short," which was a term used by soldiers to let others know that someone would be leaving Vietnam very soon. I know the day after I arrived in Charlie Company, like every other soldier in Vietnam, I started counting the days I had left. Often, guys would ask if you were getting short. I might, for example, say 212 days or 198 days. Everyone knew what you meant because everyone wanted to be short so they could go home.

We all hated Vietnam and everything it represented. Some guys used canes when they were short, and they'd walk around LZ Bayonet with them. They called them short-timer sticks. Their faces would be beaming. They really wanted everyone to know how short they were.

When I left LZ Bayonet, I was driven either to Chu Lai or Da Nang. I don't recall which. I do know that I boarded the jet and put my seatbelt on. I couldn't wait for that plane to get airborne. Once it did, every passenger let out a loud hoot. The journey back to the world had begun.

PART THREE

The World

THE PLANE STOPPED IN SEVERAL PLACES to refuel. Finally, on February 13, 1969, we landed mid-morning in Seattle, Washington. For some reason, it took a long time to deplane, and the soldiers were becoming very vocal and loud because we had to wait. Everyone was complaining about "this fucking Army" that can't get anything right. The guy next to me asked me why I wasn't upset, and I told him that I'd waited for this day for an entire year. What was fifteen more minutes? It took about that long to get things straight so that we could get off the plane. I stepped off the bottom step and touched U.S. soil for the first time in what seemed like an eternity. It was exhilarating to say the least.

We were bussed to Ft. Lewis, Washington, where we were fitted for uniforms by civilian tailors. Then, we were directed to the mess hall where we could feast on a steak. After the meal, we were given new uniforms with the appropriate ribbons, medals and name tag. After being assigned our new duty station, we were officially released to go home on a thirty-day leave. I made arrangements to fly to Chicago and then on to Oshkosh, Wisconsin.

When I arrived in Oshkosh, no one knew I was coming. My parents, who'd been expecting me on the 17th and not the 13th of February, were still on vacation in Florida. I was in a bit of a daze. Twenty-four hours earlier I'd been in Vietnam and here I was back in Wisconsin. Instead of calling a brother or sister or friend to pick me up, I called a taxi. Throughout that year in Vietnam, to a great extent, I'd become depersonalized because of all of my experiences there. I really did not want to deal with anyone. The taxi driver picked me up. I put my luggage in the trunk and got in the back seat. After I gave him my destination, he noticed my tanned face and asked if I'd been to Florida. I said, "No. Vietnam." Not another word was exchanged between us until we arrived at my home and he told me the fare. I didn't feel normal.

Culture Shock

I'D BEEN GONE SO LONG THAT MY PERSONAL relationship skills were greatly diminished. I was probably clinically depressed; but at that time, there was no debriefing time or acculturation time for soldiers returning from Vietnam. We got on a plane from Vietnam and then flew back to American cities and, within twenty-four hours, we were expected to resume our lives.

It became apparent very early on, as I tried to mix with family and friends, that our frame of reference about things was very different. It seemed that all of these people had changed while I was away. How did that happen? It didn't occur to me for a very long time that I was the one who had changed. And how I had changed!

For the first week of my leave, I visited my high school and met some former teachers. I tried to explain to them what Vietnam was all about. But after a short time, I could tell they weren't all that interested. As time went on, I felt that I was failing in my relationships with my friends. I even alienated some of them. It didn't take long for me to realize that I could not handle being home.

So I called my buddy, Al Torsiello, who had arrived home in Union, New Jersey, a few weeks before I got home. I told him my situation, and he understood completely. He said, "Doc, I'm having the same problems." He asked me to fly out. I quickly made arrangements, hooked up with Al and stayed at his house. He came from an Italian family, a brother and two sisters. Also, he had a wonderful father—I wondered how he got so lucky— and the sweetest mother in the world. I was welcomed into Al's family as if I were one of them. They all called me Jimmy, the only people who did that. Al still called me Doc. His father stocked the liquor cabinet and the refrigerator in the basement. He had only one rule for us. Don't drink and leave the house. So each evening Al and I would walk down to the basement and talk through the war over an enormous amount of vodka and beer. Despite the hangovers, we both felt much better. The bond between us had been rekindled. Al and I were Vietnam brothers. Finally, I had someone in the States I could relate to.

Savannah, Georgia

I HAD EIGHTEEN MONTHS REMAINING in the Army and was stationed at the Tuttle Army Air Base Hospital in Savannah. I was assigned to the surgery clinic there and worked with three wonderful doctors: Doctor Baker, the hospital administrator; Dr. Murphy; and Dr. Ibarra. My job was to assist all three of these doctors with any surgical matter that could be handled in our clinic. We served soldiers as well as their civilian dependents. An example of how I would assist would be if one of the doctors removed, say, a sebaceous cyst, he would tell me, "Jim, sew him up." All three of these doctors had tremendous confidence in my abilities. It didn't take long for me to get very accomplished at suturing. I enjoyed this work a lot. The doctors often complimented me on my skills and said that I could do the suturing as well as they did. After my eight-hour day at the clinic, I would often venture down to the emergency room and ask if anyone needed to be sewed up. It wasn't unusual for a soldier to get into a bar fight and come in needing sutures.

One day I was called into a meeting with one of the surgeons in our Surgical Clinic, and he asked me to sit in with him while he consulted with a middle-aged woman, a civilian dependent. As softly as he could, he told her that she had breast cancer. He recommended a mastectomy. He discussed with her the operation and the after-care. When she left, I asked the surgeon what her chances of survival were. He said, "We can only hope for the best."

On the day of the mastectomy, I scrubbed up and assisted with the surgery. A blue line was drawn around the breast and the surgical knife was handed to me. The doctor said, "Jim, now begin cutting at the point and go through the skin about a quarter of an inch and follow the blue line." I did as I was instructed. Then I was told to continue cutting a little deeper this time. Again, I did as I was told. I realized that I was not at all squeamish. Compared to my Vietnam experience, this operation was less severe and more clinical in nature. I was fully immersed in what I was doing. I did some more cutting and then the surgeon took over and finished the surgery. He bandaged the area and then the patient was taken to post-op. A few days after the surgery, I visited the woman on the ward, spoke with her and wished her the best of luck with the after-care.

When she checked out several days later, I figured I'd never see her again.

****

One day in the Surgical Clinic, one of the surgeons asked me what I was going to do when I got out of the Army. I told him I'd probably go to college, and he asked if I'd considered medical school. I told him that I hadn't. At this point in my life, I hadn't set the bar that high for myself. Also, I didn't think I was smart enough or qualified enough for medical school. The surgeon said if I ever changed my mind, he'd pay my way through medical school. I don't know what my response was, but I know I was truly and deeply honored that he had such confidence in my abilities.

But I was still in the Army and had to contend with all that I had to do before I could think about what I'd do when I got out. Without a doubt, my attitude towards the military had suffered.

For one thing, I no longer adhered to the military spit-shine mentality. At this time, I was a hospital corpsman, so I pushed the boundaries by letting my hair and sideburns grow. I stopped wearing my name tag. And, instead of the black military dress shoes, I wore penny loafers. None of these decisions on my part endeared me to the non-commissioned career soldiers that vets called lifers, a derogatory term which meant we didn't think these guys could make it outside the military. We used the term often and sometimes directly. These guys were not combat vets. They held a rank higher than mine simply because of the length of their service. A few of these guys tried to cause problems for me; but as long as Colonel Baker was the hospital administrator, and I worked directly for him, they couldn't lay a hand on me.

In the spring of 1970, when Colonel Baker was on a two-week leave, I received a transfer from the Surgical Clinic to the second floor. I was handed a mop by a lifer who didn't like me and was told to mop the floors. When I was done washing them, I was to polish and buff them. I was in the Army, so I did it, though reluctantly. For the next two weeks, I got every shit job that could be handed out.

In addition to these menial jobs, though, I also had ward responsibilities, which meant I had to stop in and check the vitals of the patients in each room, change bed pans, move patients and do all of the things I had been trained to do in Ft. Sam Houston, Texas.

On the second floor, the woman whose mastectomy I had assisted with checked in. She was feeling poorly, so we did our best to make her comfortable. I was told she didn't have much time to live. I checked in on her often to make sure we were doing everything possible to make her last days easier. One day I stopped in only to find that she had just died. I checked her pulse, and there was none. I contacted the nurse on duty, and she came down and confirmed that my friend had passed away. A doctor was then called in to make the death determination, and I was then told to prepare the patient for transfer to the funeral home. That's when it dawned on me that I had come full circle with this patient, from the initial consult with the surgeon to the mastectomy, to visiting and caring for her on the second floor in her final days, to finding her dead in her room and packing her oral cavities for transfer to the funeral home. Although my emotions had been stunted by what I had seen and experienced in Vietnam, to the extent that I could feel compassion for another person, I genuinely felt it for her.

When Dr. Baker returned from his two-week leave and found that I had been transferred, he got me back to the Surgical Clinic. Not long after this, the colonel in administration had been reviewing my personal file, probably for my promotion to E-5 medical specialist. He discovered in my file that I had received military orders for the Silver Star but that it had never been formally awarded or presented to me. When the colonel left, Dr. Murphy asked if that was true. I said it was but that it didn't matter to me because I couldn't care less if I got it. I told him that I was more proud of the combat medical badge that I had received.

Colonel Baker became aware of the administrative snafu, and he immediately called the commanding general at the post and explained the situation. He told me to go home and put on my dress greens and report to the Sergeant Major, the highest ranking enlisted military man at our hospital. I did what I was told. The Sergeant Major commented in a negative fashion about the length of my hair and said it looked like I had polished my shoes with a chocolate bar. After telling me I looked like a bum, he sent me to the General's office. Then I was awarded the Silver Star. Photographers were there taking pictures but none appeared in the newsletter, though an article did. I assumed that someone had determined that I didn't give off the proper military appearance and didn't want my picture in the newsletter. My attitude was such at the time that I really didn't give a shit.

This cynical military attitude of mine continued to worsen. I started checking out university schedules and found that Wisconsin State University (now the University of Wisconsin, Oshkosh) in my home town had summer classes that would begin in early June 1970. I had attended a local college while in Savannah, Armstrong State College, and took an Introduction to Psychology course. I'd gotten my initial taste of college there. I'd also taken advantage of the College Level Examination Program (CLEP) while in the Army and accrued six social studies credits. Despite my high school guidance counselor telling me I wasn't college material, I decided I'd give it a try anyway.

In May 1970, I went to see Dr. Baker and told him a white lie, that I was thinking of going to medical school and needed to get a start on it because I was now twenty-one years old. He asked when my classes would start. When I said they'd begin on June 3, he called in his secretary and dictated a letter to her saying I was to get out of the Army within a week. He did me a huge favor. I was thrilled to leave the Army on June 1, 1970, with an early out.

University of
Wisconsin, Oshkosh

I BEGAN COLLEGE IN THE SUMMER OF 1970 taking seven credits. Though I did well in all of my courses, I just didn't feel comfortable in that environment. As is already well known, because of the Vietnam War, the country had turned against the veterans who fought there. That feeling was pervasive all over the United States, but it was especially strong on college campuses. Like many other veterans, I withdrew and became isolated. After what we'd been through, all we wanted was to fit in and be like everyone else. I was in classes with eighteen-year-olds who were still living with their parents. These kids were so immature that I could not relate to them. Though I was only a few years older than they were, I felt like their parents.

Veterans on campus sought out other veterans. Given my experience, I looked for other combat veterans. Soon, I discovered a group of combat vets who had been hanging out at Terry's, a local bar. In our isolation, we used alcohol and pot to self-medicate. While I was hanging out with the vets at Terry's, I was determined to get through college as quickly as I could. In two years and nine months, I did just that. The reason I was able to accomplish my goal in such a short time was because I had accrued credits while in the military. Also, I was awarded credits—in anatomy, physiology and health and safety—for being a medic and a veteran. Not only that but I attended classes in summers and between semesters.

My bother Dic, who was a Marine in Vietnam, attended the same university that I did. We'd take the same classes. If they met three times a week, Dic would go one day and take notes; and I'd go on another day and do the same. Then we'd skip the third class. Somehow we both made it out of undergraduate school in 1973 with degrees in education. What's interesting about going to school with Dic (who got out of the military as part of the McNamara withdrawals in 1970) is that he and I seldom discussed Vietnam. To this date, with the exception of a few letters we sent to each other, we talked about the war maybe five times. It is just not a subject we have opened up about.

Despite our reticence on the subject, we both somehow got on with our lives. After a few years on the road playing music with my former high school bandmate, Paul Muetzel, I went back to UWO and received a Master's degree in Guidance Counseling in 1978.

Heading East

I THEN MOVED EAST AND GOT A JOB IN Salisbury, Maryland, assisting disabled veterans in finding jobs. After thoroughly interviewing the guys and becoming very well versed in their particular skill set, I would then search out companies that did the kind of work that went along with their skills. Often there were advantages to companies in hiring disabled vets, so I was able to find jobs for many of them. Though I enjoyed the work, the pay was very low. What I wanted was to get a higher-paying job with the federal government.

Eventually, I landed a job with the Defense Logistics Agency in Alexandria, Virginia, on a veteran's readjustment appointment, a program designed to employ some Vietnam veterans in federal jobs. While working in Alexandria, I heard about the first Vietnam Veteran Counseling Center to be opened in the entire country in Washington, D.C., so I went there and volunteered my services on several occasions. It was as therapeutic for me as it was for other veterans to be able to talk about what went on in Vietnam and how it had impacted our lives. It helped a lot that we were able to do this in a safe environment staffed by Vietnam veterans.

At the Vietnam Veterans Counseling Center, I also read the first major book published on PTSD. What hit home the most for me was what the author, Dr. Wilson, said about his feeling the most empathy for those soldiers who were combat medics ill-prepared for the circumstances and misery that they faced in Vietnam. After reviewing the symptoms of PTSD, I realized that most of them applied to me, my brother, my friend Al and almost every combat veteran I knew. None of us, to my knowledge, applied for benefits related to PTSD through the Veterans Administration, which finally accepted it as a diagnosis in the 1970s, probably in large part because of Dr. Wilson's work.

When I think about Wilson's comment and my work as a medic, I go back to a particular day when I was in Vietnam with the infantry. On that day, while on a short break, I said to some of my infantry buddies, "You guys are the lowest on the Army rung and you have the most horrible jobs. I wonder if people back in the world realize this." One infantry guy looked at me and said, "Do you want to know who really has the worst job in the Army?" I shook my head no because in my mind I felt I already knew the answer: it was the grunts. He then said, "You!" All the guys in that group nodded their heads in agreement. This was a revelation to me because I had such tremendous respect for what they did, these amazingly brave grunts. These were "my guys" and I had become very protective of them. Until that exchange about our jobs, I had no idea that these tough bastards believed without a doubt that my job was tougher than theirs. Dr. Wilson and these guys were on the same page.

Being a medic with the infantry was a horrible job, but what made it even worse was that I did not receive the training that I should have gotten. Still, I did the best I could. I can honestly say that I gave it my all.

Assimilation and Resurgence

V IETNAM VETERANS IN THE 1970s assimilated back into society pretty much on their own. They didn't talk to others about their service in the war because most people didn't want to hear it. Americans turned their backs on us. At that time, the country could not separate the hugely unpopular Vietnam War from the warriors. In fact, people for whom I had no respect—like Bill Ayers and his sort—gained more attention for bombing institutions within our own country than the Vietnam vets did who did what they were ordered to do.

Until the Iran hostages were released in January 1981, the country treated Vietnam veterans with very little respect. When the hostages were released, the country began celebrating. People wrapped trees in yellow ribbons in neighborhoods throughout the land. The country was ebullient with the news. Soon, welcome-home parades were held in the hometowns of the hostages.

These parades were widely covered in the national media. I remember one reporter who looked to someone in the crowd and said, "I wonder what the Vietnam veterans think of this?" That question resonated, and soon the cover of *Time* magazine read: "Vietnam Veterans Fighting for their Rights."

That magazine cover started some dialogue about Vietnam, a subject that was very unpopular. Slowly, people realized that those of us who answered the call, either voluntarily or through the draft, were not bad people. Rather, we were regular guys who found ourselves fighting in an extremely long and unpopular war. It took awhile, but the American people have finally been able to separate the war from the warrior.

Many of us warriors who have survived are, to some degree, still dealing with the after-effects of that hellish war. Initially, I began writing about my experience just as an exercise which I found therapeutic. Soon, I found myself typing as quickly as my fingers would hit the keys. During this process, I never had writer's block. The words just flowed out effortlessly, almost like they were being forced out of me. Perhaps they were.

When I realized that writing my story was therapeutic, I saved what I had written on that first day and titled it "Cleansing My Soul." I thought I'd just leave it there and pick it up again sometime later. I gave it this title because I felt that, in some ways, I had been "dirtied up" in the war. Also, I felt that I needed to see on the printed page some of the things I'd been ashamed of for so many years. My thought was that I would see them there on the page, absorb them and then delete them; and no one would be the wiser.

Then, I got busy on another project and forgot about my writing exercise until several months later. I was looking at the document section of my computer and saw the file called "Cleansing My Soul." When I opened the file, I realized what was before me. I decided I had to write more. I spent many hours writing non-stop and doing very little editing. It became increasingly clear to me that I had to write this story, not because my experience had been that much different from any other combatant—others surely had it worse than I did—but because I own this story.

It wasn't long before I had finished fifty single-spaced pages.

That's when I started to think about publishing my story as an e-book. I had never written a book before, but I saw no reason not to continue writing with that goal in mind. I knew that Vietnam memoirs were beginning to come back into the marketplace. Also, with Ken Burns' documentary, "Vietnam 2016," in the organizational stage, maybe the time would be right for an ordinary Vietnam veteran to write an e-book. So I wrote on.

What I discovered in writing a book about war is that I never found the right words to describe my constant fear. I couldn't find the right words to describe the bloody, grotesque wounds I had seen. How was I to tell a reader what it feels like to think I was going to die at any moment, not once but many times over? I didn't know how to convey what it felt like to walk through what we believed to be a mine field thinking each careful step could be my last. How was I to tell others what it was like to lie to a soldier and tell him he was going to live when I knew there was no chance?

The words I settled on in my story to give readers some inkling as to what I experienced in Vietnam may not capture the horror that I witnessed as precisely as I'd like it to. But it's my hope that you can get some sense of it and, thus, have a better understanding of what we went through over there. Combat veterans had long periods of inactivity and then, when the shit hit the fan, our fear and terror levels went off the charts. We were all so young. The average age of combatants in our unit may have been nineteen. We were kids who became hardened adults. I don't know how anyone who goes through combat on the ground can come out unchanged. The maturation process with infantrymen was like a speeding bullet. There was no time to grow up naturally.

My own war experience impacted me emotionally and physically. Still today, if I hear the sound of a firecracker, I have startle reflex, which means I duck my head. I can't shake it. Since the war, I have been very hardened. It's extremely difficult for me to express personal feelings. I've been somehow emotionally stunted by the horrors I witnessed over there. Physically, I had stress-related issues; and my back is full of arthritis, some of which I attribute to my year in Vietnam.

When I smell blood, I link it to gunpowder, something a normal person does not do. These are personal things. It's important to remember that every veteran's story is personal. The specifics may vary from soldier to soldier, but it's always the case that our stories are personal. We live with them and in them as best we can as we get on with our lives, forever marked by what we saw. Think about the nineteen-year-olds that you know. The next time you look at them, imagine a dangerous weapon in their hands, 14,000 miles from home, moving around in jungles in a war zone trying to stay alive. That was me, my friend Al and countless others. We were just kids.

I know there are many other veterans out there who were only nineteen when they joined up or were drafted. At that young age, they too were given a gun and dropped off in a jungle to fight for our country. Writing about such an experience is one thing, bringing it into the public eye quite another. What finally motivated me to not only write but to publish my story was, first and foremost, the possibility that I might inspire other veterans to open up about their own Vietnam experiences. What each of you did over there—what you risked, the horrors that you witnessed—is vital to our nation's history; but, more importantly, it's vital to you personally. There's no question that the younger generation needs to understand the big historical picture of that long and bloody war. But I strongly believe that it's just as important for young people to get a sense of the many personal histories that make up the larger one. Without these individual stories, the history of the Vietnam War is incomplete. No matter what your particular story is, remember that you own it; and only you can tell it the way it needs to be told.

I wrote this book to share my personal story and to honor the greatest men I have ever known—my fellow infantrymen. I want to honor them, and their names come largely from my memory and lists I came upon. I sincerely apologize if I missed someone. Besides the names of soldiers previously mentioned in this book who tragically were killed, these honorable men include the following:

Jame Allie, Gary Amberson, Anthony Angeles, Richard Arrington, Richard Arthur, Gene Ashe, Frank Baumgardner. Fred Belcher, Ray Biathrow, Dave Bliss. Tom Boeckman, Alan Bradley, Charles Bush, Joseph Buss, Daniel Busse, Tom Cameron, Michael Carl, Ernie Carrier, Richard Castillo, Manuel Chavarria, Jr., David Christiansen, Bill Chupp, John Clapp,III, Richard Claverlie, Ray Clinton, Garry Cobb, Thomas Collins, William Cooper, Henry Courbis, Jr., Cyril Corrigan, James Cowell, Paul Cullinane, Jr., Gary Daly, Mark Deam, David Desjardins, Paul Del Vitto, Danny Dingus, John Dykty, Clyde Elmore, Gene Emigh, Raymond Estrada, Leroy Ferguson, Michael Filbin, John Foley, Tony Funtanilla, Pierre Gagnon, Don Gilliland, Delvis Godwin, Luis Gomez-Mesa, Alberto Gonzalez, Wallace Gordon, Gary Grechika, Charles Griffin, III, William "Bunk" Halunen, Rene Hamann, Robert E. Harris, Robert G. Harris, Doug Harrison, Clarence Hepburn, Jr., Darl Herlocker, John Hill, Jr., John Hooper, John Hovey, Melvin Hudson, Tom Hume, John Hurtado, Terry Ivey, Ray Jackson, Gary Jacobson, John James, Fred Jolly, David Jones, Ted Joslin, Robert Kaloostian, Delmar Katmer, Jim Kelleher, Calvin Kelly,

Nicholas Kenlaw, Charlie Kennerly, III, William Kleeman, Jr., James Kline, Thomas Knezevic, Clifford Knight, John Koger, David Kral, Lonnie Laws, Robert Lees, Jr., Bill Lobeck, Jim Loman, Douglas Loy, Eugene Lynch, Robert Madson, Sauilamau Maene, Sam Maggio, Charles Majer, Leonard Marshall, Jr., James Maurer, Robert Mayer, Ed McCracken, Jack McLaughlin, Allen McPherson, Tom Medlin, Jr., Lawrence Miller, Mark Morgan, Richard Morris, Michael Murnin, Joe Murphree, Glenn Myers, Mike Myers, Mike Nanton, Earl Odom, Tim O'Donnell, Steve Ohara, Angel "Gypsy" Ortiz, Louie Panteleone, Bruce Parker, James Parks, Neal Paulshock, Joe Pascale, Don Peterson, Donald Pickney, Herman Pierce, George Powell, Jr., Walter Pratt, Gary Pratt, David Provost, Stephen Pye, Reynaldo Quintana, Marco Rea, Dan Reid, Tom Rizzo, Wade Rodland II, Artenio Romero, Jr., Hobert Salisbury, Gary Samuels, Johnnie Schaffer, Joe Schwartz, Bob Scott, Jeff Segal, William Shelton, Roger Shrewsberry, William Sicknick, Melvin Spencer, Paul Spiro, Jim Stringham, Glenn Strombach, James Stark, Debarry Stewart, Richard Stowe, David Tank, Clifton Taylor, Andrew Thomas, Richard Tolentino, Roger Tolson, Vale Torres, Alan Torsiello, Gary Tricamo, Howard Vadasz, John Venegoni, Heinrich Vollmano, Joe Walsh, Robert Washington, George Welsh, Ward Westerberg, John Wetsel, Gary Wheeler, Tyrone Williams, Jesse Willoughby, Michael Wilson, Ray Witzke, and Robert Zimmerman.

Author's Note

W HEN I COMPLETED MY YEAR OF SERVICE IN Vietnam in 1969, I told myself that it was over. I never wanted to think about the war again. How young and naive I was! In fact, the war has never left me and, at times, it almost consumed me. I now know that it will be with me until my final breath.

I never expected to write a book about my Vietnam service. Had I planned on writing such a book, I would have taken down some notes or saved a lot of photographs. I did neither. What I did do one day in 2017 was sit down at my computer and start writing about the war. Much to my surprise, the stories came out faster than I could type. And I wrote and wrote. When I finished, I read it and said to myself that I have gotten all of this horror and sadness and some shame out of my system, so I can just delete it and consider the process as therapeutic. Instead, I let some Vietnam vets read it, including Al Torsiello who served with me in my platoon in Vietnam, and they encouraged me to publish it. So, this book is based, to the extent possible, on historical accuracy; but it is completely drawn from my memory almost fifty years after the fact.

Truth cuts to the bone. Some of what's written here is hard for me to read and difficult to share. In this book, I hold a mirror to my life and then let the chips fall where they may. I describe my life as a nineteen-year-old kid, 14,000 miles away from home during 1968/69, possibly the most turbulent time in American history since the Civil War. I want the reader to understand that some decisions I made back then were because I frankly didn't think I would survive the war. I fully expected to be seriously injured or killed, so I made some decisions that I may not have made under different circumstances because I didn't want to miss out on the opportunity to experience some things. I decided to write it all...and truth sometimes can be ugly.

About the Author

J IM PURTELL IS AN ACTIVIST FOR VIETNAM veterans, particularly those who had been left behind, the prisoners of war/missing in action (POW/MIAs) in Southeast Asia. Using his songwriting abilities, he put together a CD of original songs about the POW/MIA experience. According to Vietnam musicologists Hugo Keesing and John Baky, he is the only known songwriter to have written a collection of songs about POW/MIAs.

When video became popular, Jim co-produced and funded a video to go along with one of these songs ("The Waiting Goes On"). The video, which can be found on YouTube, was shot at the birthplace of his mother in Ashipun, Wisconsin, on the very farm where she grew up.

Jim also co-produced a video about his uncle's service in Korea and interwove it with his Vietnam service. This video, also on YouTube, is called "Forgotten No More." The song was written by Purtell and Ricki E. Bellos.

He, Bellos and Al Torsiello wrote a collection of songs based on his and Torsiello's service in Vietnam. It's called "Vietnam: There and Back" and can be found at www.vietnamthereandback.com.

Jim also funded and co-produced a provocative video about Agent Orange. It features a Bellos/Purtell song called "Dear Agent Orange." This video can also be found on YouTube.

WWW.HELLAGATEPRESS.COM